The Trinity among the Nations

The Doctrine of God in the Majority World

Edited by

Gene L. Green, Stephen T. Pardue, K. K. Yeo

Langham

GLOBAL LIBRARY

This book is published in cooperation with Wm. B. Eerdmans Publishing Co., Grand Rapids. First published in 2015 by Wm. B. Eerdmans Publishing Co., ISBN: 978-0-8028-7268-5 (North American edition)

This edition published in 2015 by Langham Global Library
an imprint of Langham Creative Projects

Langham Partnership
PO Box 296, Carlisle, Cumbria
CA3 9WZ, UK
www.langham.org

ISBNs:
978-1-78368-105-1 Print
978-1-78368-134-1 Mobi
978-1-78368-133-4 ePub
978-1-78368-135-8 PDF

British Library Cataloguing in Publication Data
A catalogue record for this book is available from the British Library

ISBN: 978-1-78368-105-1

Cover art: © Baptism of Jesus by He Qi
www.heqiart.com

Langham Partnership actively supports theological dialogue and a scholar's right to publish but does not necessarily endorse the views and opinions set forth, and works referenced within this publication or guarantee its technical and grammatical correctness. Langham Partnership does not accept any responsibility or liability to persons or property as a consequence of the reading, use or interpretation of its published content.

Contents

Abbreviations

1 En.	*1 Enoch*
4 Esd.	*4 Esdras*
ABC	Anchor Bible Commentary
BNTC	Black's New Testament Commentary
FRLANT	Forschungen zur Religion und Literatur des Alten und Neuen Testaments
Gen. Rab.	*Genesis Rabbah*
HTKNT	Herders Theologischer Kommentar zum Neuen Testament
ICC	International Critical Commentary
Leg. all.	Philo, *Legum allegoriae*
JSNT	*Journal for the Study of the New Testament*
JSNTSup	Journal for the Study of the New Testament Supplement series
LXX	Septuagint
MT	Masoretic Text
NIGTC	New International Greek Testament Commentary
PNTC	Pillar New Testament Commentary
Quaest. in Gen.	Philo, *Quaestiones et solutiones in Genesin*
Vit. Cont.	Philo, *De vita contemplativa*
WBC	Word Biblical Commentary

To MJ △ discussion

Stop engaging/focussing on US evangelicalism a fading Western church ~ engage with global Xty.

Trinity 101: Kaleidoscopic Views of God in the Majority World

K. K. YEO

Christianity has made a unique claim among world religions: God is one, and there are three persons (Father, Son, and Spirit) who are God. In the Christology volume of this Majority World Theology series,[1] scholars from the global church present a thesis that God is Christlike. Yet much more can be said about God. In this volume, the thesis advanced is: God is one and trinitarian — but this is more easily asserted than proved. Indeed, "one is in danger of losing [one's] soul by denying the Trinity and of losing [one's] wits by trying to understand it"[2] — but believe and understand we must. Our understanding of this doctrine has great consequences for how we apprehend who God is and how God works in history; it also has rich implications for how we understand who we are as God's creatures, who we are as a church, and what Christian ministry, mission, and spiritual life entail.

This introductory chapter serves as a guide to help readers study this doctrine, and to avoid studying it in isolation or from an exclusively Western perspective.[3] We invite you to sit at a round-table with

---

1. See the first volume of this series: Gene L. Green, Stephen Pardue, and K. K. Yeo, eds., *Jesus without Borders*, Majority World Theology (Grand Rapids: Eerdmans, 2014).

2. Bruce M. Stephens, *God's Last Metaphor: The Doctrine of the Trinity in New England Theology* (Ann Arbor: Scholars Press, 1981), p. 75. Or Augustine: "If you can understand it, it is not God."

3. Basic texts from the Western perspectives abound; I recommend a few: Alister McGrath, *Christian Theology: An Introduction*, 3rd ed. (Malden, Mass.: Blackwell, 2001); Colin E. Gunton, *Father, Son and Holy Spirit: Essays Toward a Fully Trinitarian Theology* (Lon-

nine biblical and theological scholars from the Majority World church. The gifts they bring are more than their academic qualifications and areas of expertise. They offer perspectives as Christian believers who breathe the air and drink the water of their homelands, live in the sociopolitical and cultural contexts of their countries, and serve their local churches and communities. These scholars, who hold diverse perspectives on scriptural reading, creedal understanding, and who God is and how God relates to their life-worlds, are committed to honest discourse. Their works are invaluable to us as we seek a clearer and fuller understanding of the basic issues of this foundational confession of our faith. While it should be clear that there are diverse understandings of the Trinity even within evangelical Western scholarship and that in the Majority World, the editors of this series are not "theological policemen." Rather, our task is to bring the global church to theological dialogue regarding kaleidoscopic understandings of the Trinity, but a dialogue that is bound and strengthened by our evangelical faithfulness to Scripture and tradition as well as our dynamic contexts.

I. Why Study the Trinity?

The liturgical contexts and doxological purposes in the formation of the Holy Scriptures, Christian creeds, and theological endeavors speak volumes about the significance of this study. Surely, the study of the Trinity is not simply an academic exercise; admittedly, it is a complex doctrine. The human quest to know how things look in light of the triune God is noble. Since "faith seeks understanding" (*fides quaerens intellectum* according to Anselm), Christian life is most fruitful when it is informed and renewed by our knowledge of God.

The Latin phrase *lex orandi, lex credendi, lex vivendi* ("the law of prayer/worship, the law of belief, the law of living") summarizes well the way our worship life informs how we believe and live.[4] Since we become what we worship — "for ruin or for restoration"[5] — it is important to pursue

---

don: T&T Clark, 2001); R. Kendall Soulen, *The Divine Name(s) and the Holy Trinity*, vol. 1, *Distinguishing the Voices* (Louisville: Westminster John Knox, 2011).

4. See also the discussion of Miroslav Volf and Michael Welker regarding the significance of trinitarian life in their *God's Life in Trinity* (Minneapolis: Fortress, 2006).

5. G. K. Beale, *We Become What We Worship: A Biblical Theology of Idolatry* (Downers

the knowledge of God in order to know God more certainly (in creed) and fully (in worship), thus grounding the ethical and ecclesial bearing of believers to live in the trinitarian life of God for God's glory and for the good of the world. The end of Christian theology is the beginning of doxology — a worship of the triune God that carries the following life-currency:

1. to restore who we are as the *imago Dei* in Christ by the Spirit;
2. to transform who we are as the body of Christ in the world for the reign of truth (authenticity), love (justice), and beauty (power);[6] and
3. to envision all of creation as children of God as they live in the divine economy/community of ecological diversity in unity, mutual hospitality, and interdependence.

All nine essays in this volume are written out of such passion for the topic and out of a shared commitment to the evangelical cause (the gospel of Christ) and to interpreting all life events through this theology (the triune God). This allegedly abstract, seemingly useless, but truly transcendent doctrine may in fact be "a practical doctrine with radical consequences for Christian life."[7]

II. Whither Trinity?

Our nine scholars are part of a revival of the study of the doctrine of the Trinity in the twentieth and twenty-first centuries. A sketch of the current landscape of various trinitarian views below will help us locate the terrain of the eight main chapters in this volume.[8]

Grove, Ill.: IVP Academic, 2008): "What people revere, they resemble, either for ruin or for restoration." See Rom. 1:20-28; 1 Cor. 10:14-22.

6. See Stephen M. Garrett, *God's Beauty-in-Act: Participating in God's Suffering Glory* (Eugene, Ore.: Pickwick, 2013).

7. Catherine Mowry LaCugna, *God for Us: The Trinity and Christian Life* (San Francisco: HarperSanFrancisco, 1991), p. ix. See, however, Thomas H. McCall's caution that "Trinitarian theology should not conflate Trinitarian doctrine with sociopolitical theological agendas" (*Which Trinity? Whose Monotheism? Philosophical and Systematic Theologians on the Metaphysics of Trinitarian Theology* [Grand Rapids: Eerdmans, 2010], pp. 224-27). Even so, his conclusion on pp. 246-53 regarding the understanding of the God-world relation is insightful.

8. The list has not included those views in the Old and New Testaments, the creedal formulations of this doctrine by the Latin and Greek fathers, and those be-

The debate of immanent and transcendent understanding of the Trinity seems to occupy the mind of the European scholars. Related issues are the relationship between Trinity and Christology (Karl Barth, N. T. Wright), person and nature (T. F. Torrance), history and revelation (Wolfhart Pannenberg), person and community (Jürgen Moltmann, John Zizioulas), and immutability and change (Richard Bauckham). Taking a step further than the European scholarship, North American scholars wrestle with the social and relative models of the Trinity. Major themes that have surfaced in their deliberation are identity and narrative (Robert Jenson, Michael Rea), God for us (Catherine M. LaCugna, Gerald Bray), God in relationship to Wisdom/Sophia (Elizabeth Johnson), Friend (Sallie McFague), or the Holy Spirit (Steven M. Studebaker).

Latin American scholars, however, take their lived experience as a necessary lens for focusing on the communal understanding of Trinity. While their concerns regarding the Trinity are not antagonistic to that of the North Atlantic region, their formulations give rich nuances to our understanding of the Trinity in the context of justice. Leonardo Boff uses the language of a perichoretic community of equals; Justo L. González speaks of a Trinity of minority; and José Míguez Bonino mentions the Trinity at work in community. Antonio González, a writer in this volume, writes of act of love as God's essence, whereas Rosalee Velloso Ewell, another writer in this volume, celebrates the reign of the Trinity in community through the Spirit.

A highly contextual theology of the Trinity is seen in the works of African scholars as well. Common themes in the African Trinity have to do with God in light of African traditional religions (John Mbiti) and Parent ancestor (Charles Nyamiti). Our African writer in this volume, Samuel Waje Kunhiyop, recounts an African Trinity in the African Orthodox and Islamic contexts.

Asian scholars have considered the significance of their indigenous worldviews and the multireligious contexts. Natee Tanchanpongs's essay reviews and assesses, for example, Jung Young Lee's yin-yang philosophical understanding of Trinity, Brahmabandhab Upadhyay's Hindu

---

fore the twentieth century. For more, see Stanley Grenz, *Rediscovering the Triune God: The Trinity in Contemporary Theology* (Minneapolis: Fortress, 2004); McCall, *Which Trinity? Whose Monotheism?*; and Stephen R. Holmes, *The Quest for the Trinity: The Doctrine of God in Scripture, History and Modernity* (Downers Grove, Ill.: IVP Academic, 2012).

religious categories *(Sat, Cit, Ananda)*, and Nozomu Miyahira's relational and communal language (Trinity as Three Betweenness and One Concord). The other two essays are more constructive: Atsuhiro Asano discusses the motherly relatedness and care of God in the Pauline Epistles and in the experience of Japanese Christians; Zi Wang revisits the challenge of translating the name of God as *Shang-ti* and *Shin*, and she then uses Paul's cross-cultural hermeneutic to suggest a way forward.

There are exciting voices emerging from the margins. The Kairos Palestine Document claims the promise of the gracious God in the land and its suffering people, and the Rainbow Spirit Elders and Aborigines in Australia call God to be their Creator Spirit. Randy Woodley's essay in this volume represents the struggle of many Native American Christians in embracing God and all creations, and asks what it means to name God as *Uhahetaqua, Atanati, Usquahula*.

Theologians in the West keep revising, and at times departing from, their own classical formulations of this doctrine.[9] Scholars from the Majority World who seek fidelity to the doctrine find that their new linguistic and cultural contexts compel them to think anew. At times, their stance seems critical and reactionary, and at other times their constructive theologies show originality coupled with continuity. Among themselves they also find nuances and disagreements; thus the need for dialogue and debate with each other.

The answer to the question "whither Trinity?" has over the centuries been contingent on the "threeness-oneness problem" and on defining more precisely key terms such as "one," "three," "person"/ *prosōpon/persona*, and "essence"/"nature"/"substance"/*ousia*. Most of the essays in this volume discuss these issues. Part of the challenge is using a limited linguistic tool to depict God, who is incomparable. How can a line, being a one-dimensional tool, depict a cube, which is a three-dimensional reality? Although languages are metaphorical and creative, analogy still falls short of allowing us to conceptualize precisely who God is and what God does. Yet the recognition that language is inadequate does not mean that we are limited to silence or to a *via negativa* (see Asano's essay). Rather, the scriptural narrative suggests that we need to deliberate more, speak more, and consult more languages for a fuller understanding (see the essays by Woodley, Wang, and Velloso Ewell).

9. See Holmes, *Quest for the Trinity*, p. 24.

For example, what does it mean to say that "God is one," or to refer to "the oneness of God" (Deut. 6:4-9)? The term "one" is used not in a quantitative (numerical) sense, but in a qualitative sense to indicate the sovereignty of God in his nature, will, and action. Whether or not one accepts the existence of other gods (thus the difference between monotheism and monolatrism),[10] the oneness of God calls for exclusive devotion to God *alone,* who is *most sovereign* above all (Isa. 45:23; 1 Cor. 8:1-6). I propose that the biblical faith is one of *soteriological* monotheism (thus monolatrism), not primarily metaphysical or numerical monotheism. Even in Old Testament usage, the word "one" is used to express a nuanced meaning: "The Hebrew *'echad* means 'one' (Gen. 1:9; Exod. 12:49; Josh. 23:10); but also 'one and the same' (Gen. 40:5; Job 31:15); or 'only' or 'alone' (1 Kings 4:19; Josh. 6:11); or *first* (Gen. 1:5; Exod. 39:10)."[11] In other words, God is unique, one and only; "there is no other [God]" (Deut. 4:39-40) or no other like him; he is incomparable (Exod. 15:11; Ps. 35:10; Isa. 40:12-17; 44:7; 45:21-22). No class, genus, or category will fit God precisely; no language can fully describe God; there is no equal (Isa. 40:25) to God; God is the real "I am who I am" (Exod. 3:14). Anthony Thiselton correctly privileges the meaning of "one" to God's *doing*: "If 'one' carries with it an application in terms of the *one living God in action,* this is no different from the *unity of focus* in which God as Father, Son, and Holy Spirit are *one in action and self-giving* in 1 Cor. 12:4-7, where distinctive actions of Father, Son, and Spirit are also identified."[12] Thus the oneness of God entails also the *unity* of the triune God; in other words, biblical monotheism and trinitarian faith are inseparable.

As we explicate unity as "oneness," we come to another difficult term, "person." There is one God (Matt. 28:19; Deut. 6:4; Isa. 45:5; 1 Tim. 2:5), not three Gods, although the Athanasian Creed states, "The

10. Monotheism professes belief in (and worships) only one God, and that other gods are forceless idols (and therefore do not exist); monolatrism acknowledges the existence of *many* gods but allows *worship* of only one God. See the following scriptural witnesses: "the gods of the peoples are idols" (Ps. 96:5); "all gods bow down before him" (Ps. 97:7); and 1 Cor. 8 and 10 regarding whether idols have forces or not. The phrase "God is one" in Romans speaks of God's impartiality to save all through Christ, and thus is in line with soteriological/christological monotheism.

11. Anthony Thiselton, *The Hermeneutics of Doctrine* (Grand Rapids: Eerdmans, 2007), p. 461, n. 55.

12. Thiselton, *The Hermeneutics of Doctrine,* p. 462 (author's emphasis).

Father is God, the Son is God, and the Holy Spirit is God" ("*Ita deus Pater, deus Filius, deus Spiritus sanctus*"; John 6:27; Heb. 1:8). Why is the sum of three "is-es" still one? During the patristic period, the Latin/Western and Greek/Eastern churches used *substantia/ousia* ("essence/nature") to speak of the oneness of God, and *persona/prosōpon/hypostasis* ("person") to speak of the threeness of God. In our modern English usage, "person" means an individualized being with his own personality (thus Karl Barth refused to speak of God as three persons).[13] In antiquity, however (e.g., Tertullian), the Latin word *persona* (Greek: *prosōpon*) means a mask worn by an actor in performing a drama (yet the New Testament usage of *prosōpon* and *hypostasis* is nuanced beyond the concept of masking to unmasking, i.e., the understanding of roles-playing of God's being and unmasking of God's mystery; "face to face" in 1 Cor. 13:12; see Bray's essay in this volume). Simply put, in trinitarian theology the threeness of God means that the threefoldness, or three persons of the Godhead, plays three roles in history for working out the drama of redemption.

The threeness of God can sound like tritheism (a belief in three equal, closely related Gods). To avoid the error of tritheism, theologians also speak of the unity/oneness of the Trinity, which means that the Father, Son, and the Holy Spirit share the same essence/nature/*ousia* (John 10:30), honor (John 5:23), and glory (John 17:5), to the extent that they have perfect communion in will, knowledge, and love (Matt. 11:27; 1 Cor. 2:10). Yet the oneness of God is not modalism (a belief in one God who reveals himself in three forms) either. So, at the same time that it acknowledges the oneness of God, the creed holds to three persons in the Godhead, each having their own uniqueness. For example, in matters of personal relations, the Father is viewed (if not strictly, at least partly) from the perspective of begetting (Eph. 1:3;

---

13. This is a difficult topic. Karl Barth refused to use the term "person" in relation to the Father, Son, and Holy Spirit because his contemporary understanding associated "person" with personality or the I-center axis of consciousness. Instead, he uses "mode of being" *(Seinsweise)*. Barth said that there is "only one Willer and Doer that the Bible calls God," not "three divine 'I's but thrice of the one divine 'I'" (Karl Barth, *Church Dogmatics* [Edinburgh: T&T Clark, 1956-75], I/1, pp. 348, 351). But the New Testament witness is that Jesus has his own will and action (only the Son is born of the Virgin Mary, baptized at the Jordan river, suffered under Pontius Pilate, is fully divine and fully human), which is quite different from the action and will of the Father. See the following footnote.

3:14), the Son is viewed from the perspective of filiation, or being begotten (Matt. 3:17; John 19:7; Heb. 1:2-3), and the Spirit is viewed from the perspective of spiration (Ezek. 37:9; John 20:22). The three persons of God have individual differences in some responsibilities and functions (John 16:14; Phil. 2:6-11; 1 Cor. 11:3), which are undertaken with voluntary dependence and subordination (an order of priority in work rather than subordination in essence).[14] While threeness in oneness will always be a mystery (a positive, dynamic, and revelational one rather than a kept-in-the-dark mystery),[15] the term "triune" (or "three-in-one") seems to speak best of God's distinctiveness and relatedness.

I applaud the minds of the Greek and Latin fathers, whose analytical and abstract categories have helped us know God more certainly. Their gift to the church is seen in their language, which is highly philosophical and scientific, although many of the linguistic expressions they used are not found in the Bible explicitly. The church fathers were doing first-rate "cross-cultural biblical interpretation" as they employed the languages and related concepts (e.g., "unnamable and ineffable" God) of Neoplatonism and Aristotle in reading the Bible. Those cultures that do not have a language system similar to that of the West, before dismissing what the classical traditions in the West have done, need to listen to their voices since monolinguistic interpretations tend to espouse limited views and can lead to idolatrous readings. More importantly today, however, we need a similar "cross-cultural interpretation" that is true to our own contexts and vernacular categories (see Wang's and Woodley's essays). I believe that this kind of Christian hermeneutics has "saved" or fulfilled the Platonic and Aristotelian philosophies in Western civilization. Similarly, Christian theology, if done well today, will indeed have a positive effect on

14. The relationship among the three persons of the Trinity is much more complex than this would indicate; see Wolfhart Pannenberg, *Systematic Theology,* trans. Geoffrey W. Bromiley (Edinburgh: T&T Clark, 1991), 1:320: "Relations among the three persons that are defined as mutual self-distinction cannot be reduced to relations of origin in the traditional sense. The Father does not merely beget the Son. He also hands over his kingdom to him and receives it back from him. . . . The Spirit is not just breathed. He also fills the Son and glorifies him in his obedience to the Father, thereby glorifying the Father himself."

15. God is both unknowable and distinct from the world; and yet, at the same time, God is knowable in his relations with the world through Jesus (the incarnated, crucified, and resurrected one) and the Holy Spirit (the indwelling and transforming one).

our cultures when Christians are true to the triune God as they find contextual material to "incarnate" the biblical faith (see Velloso Ewell and Asano's essays).

Whither Trinity? Whatever language (which is the soul of a culture) we use, it is important to hold to monotheistic (oneness) and trinitarian (threeness) affirmations in close, healthy tension. As McCall advocates:

1. Trinitarian theology should be committed to monotheism.
2. Trinitarian theology should insist on the full divinity of the distinct persons, and it should avoid whatever might compromise the full equality and divinity of the persons.
3. Trinitarian theology should insist on an understanding of persons . . . who exist together in loving relationships of mutual dependence.[16]

Without such commitment, "God without Christ and the Spirit is remote and unavailing, Christ without God and the Spirit is a martyred saint, the Spirit without God and Christ is power bereft of form and direction. Faith lives from the interconnection of the three."[17]

A good example of this is found in Gregory of Nyssa's "On the Trinity,"[18] where he defends the idea of unity within the Godhead over the "subordinated-and-created-Son" idea of Arianism and the "imperfect-humanity-but-divine-Logos-as-Christ-soul" idea of Apollinarianism. Gregory argues that the word "Godhead" refers not to God's nature, for God's nature is unknowable and therefore cannot be expressed positively. He says that "Godhead" must refer to an operation *(energeia)* of God, which "has its origin in the Father, proceeds through the Son, and reaches its completion by the Holy Spirit. . . . Operation is not divided among the persons involved."[19] Gregory does not speak of the Godhead as three substances. Gregory accepts the threeness of God in that the three persons of the Godhead are distinct only as *hypostases*:

16. McCall, *Which Trinity? Whose Monotheism?* pp. 229-46.

17. Soulen, *Distinguishing the Voices*, p. 4.

18. In Peter C. Hodgson and Robert H. King, eds., *Readings in Christian Theology* (Philadelphia: Fortress, 1985), pp. 60-64.

19. Hodgson and King, *Readings in Christian Theology*, pp. 62-63. See Ps. 84:9; Matt. 9:4; Acts 5:3, which refer to the Father and the Son and the Holy Spirit as God respectively.

the unbegotten Father, the begotten Logos, and the proceeding Spirit. Gregory puts much emphasis on the oneness (or unity) of God in the sense that the three persons are undistinguished in essence or substance *(ousia)*.

Jürgen Moltmann, revising somewhat the Western trinitarian formulation, offers another example when he speaks of the "togetherness" of a family rather than oneness/unity of persons.[20] Likewise Leonardo Boff, a Majority World scholar from Brazil (see also González and Velloso Ewell's papers), underlines the trinitarian communion: "The Trinitarian vision produces a vision of a church that is more communion than hierarchy, more service than power, more circular than pyramidal, more loving embrace than bending the knee before authority."[21]

III. Naming the Unnamable Triune God

In naming God, we name who we are.[22] In Genesis 1, God named the world into existence, and soon Adam was gifted with the speech-act of naming other creatures and Eve, by which Adam enters into an intersubjective relationship with them. Thus theology is to speak well of God, with clarity, eloquence, and power; and theological prolegomena always involve language, especially naming God, enabling us to relate to our source and destiny. Naming is not simply a substitution of words for things they represent;[23] it is neither a magical charm nor an arbitrary, useless label. For when language is used aptly, it can lead the user to participate in the mystery of the event (i.e., the event re-presents the mystery), in this case the trinitarian life. The divine invitation for humans to contemplate and declare God's name, and

20. Jürgen Moltmann, *The Trinity and the Kingdom of God: The Doctrine of God*, trans. Margaret Kohl (London; SCM, 1981), p. 160. Cf. McCall, *Which Trinity? Whose Monotheism?* pp. 164-66.

21. Leonardo Boff, *Trinity and Society*, vol. 2, *Liberation and Theology* (London: Burns & Oates, 1988), p. 154.

22. For more, see Paul Ricoeur, "Naming God," in *Figuring the Sacred: Religion, Narrative and the Imagination*, trans. David Pellauer, ed. Mark I. Wallace (Minneapolis: Fortress, 1995), pp. 227-28.

23. The word "name" is not simply a noun; it can be verb, adjective, parable, or even narrative.

thus express divine uniqueness and action, renders people receptive to God's presence and his promised blessings.[24]

How do we name God? This is Moses' question to God: "Who shall I say sent me?" (Exod. 3:13). Exodus 3:14-15 reveals three divine names in response to Moses' query: "I am who I am," "I AM [has sent me to you]," and "YHWH" (these four Hebrew letters, referred to as the Tetragrammaton, are without vowels and therefore cannot be pronounced; thus pious Jews often use the surrogates "the Name" [*ha-Shem*] or "the LORD" [*Adonai*] instead). The locus classicus for God's transcendence *and* immanence, being *and* doing, monotheism *and* trinitarianism (or singularity and triunity), is found in these three names of God (Exod. 3:12-15) as we do a *synergic/confluencing reading* of both the Hebrew and the Greek texts within the canonical wholeness.[25]

Two points should be kept in mind at this point. First, the trinitarian monotheism ("I am who I am," "I AM," and YHWH[26]) of Exodus 3 is used repeatedly, with some variations, in regard to Jesus' claims about himself in the New Testament (see the Gospel of John, the Pauline Epistles, and Revelation especially).[27] Although the Old Testament narrates a rigorously monotheistic Israelite faith and the idea of the threeness of God is vague,[28] it is possible to think of the "divine plurals"[29] of Genesis (1:26; 3:22; 11:7) and Isaiah (6:8) as a rich resource for

24. Soulen, *Distinguishing the Voices*, pp. 133-73.

25. For more, see K. K. Yeo, "The 'Yin and Yang' of God (Exod. 3:14) and Humanity (Gen. 1:27)," *Zeitschrift für Religions- und Geistesgeschichte* 46, no. 4 (1994): 319-32.

26. See John I. Durham, *Exodus*, Word Biblical Commentary (Waco: Word, 1987), pp. 34-41, for various interpretations and literature.

27. The following New Testament texts have explicit references to Christ's preexistence: John 1:1; 8:58; 17:5; 1 Cor. 8:6; 10:4; 2 Cor. 8:9; Phil. 2:6; Col. 1:15; Heb. 1:2; ll:26; Rev. 22:13. The Gospel of John presents Christ as the Logos of God, thus implying that Jesus the Word is God. *Logos* bespeaks a divine being who is with God before time, and that Logos is God. Note how the Greek fathers' use of *Logos* resonates with the Platonic idea that sees Logos as an agent in creation and an intelligible structure immanent in nature. See Soulen's masterful treatment of this subject in *Distinguishing the Voices*, pp. 127-256.

28. E.g., the plural "divine messengers" (or angels of God; Gen. 18:2-8), or the tendency to read the trinitarian view or the idea of "majesty plural" into the word *elohim* (plural of "God" in Hebrew).

29. The God of the OT reveals himself not as a singular "I" but as a personal being whose plenitude surpasses in richness all human understanding. G. A. F. Knight calls this the "qualitative plural," meaning the diversity in unity of God. See his *A Biblical Approach to the Doctrine of the Trinity* (Edinburgh: Oliver and Boyd, 1953), p. 20.

the New Testament's trinitarian overtones. These are then further developed by the church fathers in clearer formulations of the Trinity.[30] Note, for example, the Jewish experience of *Yahweh* or *Elohim* as God the Father who *saves* through his Word *(dabar)* and the Breath/Spirit *(ruach)*.[31] Francis Watson's thick reading of Genesis 1 regarding the three distinct modes of divine creative action interprets Genesis 1: the first divine creativity is the transcendent divine command ("God said, 'Let there be light' . . . and there was light"); the second is the material involvement ("God said, 'Let there be a firmament' . . . and God made the firmament"); the third is mediation by indwelling ("God said, 'Let the earth put forth vegetation.' . . . The earth brought forth vegetation").[32] Holmes comments that "he [Watson] reads this as an account of *triune divine action*, indivisibly united, but representing the particular modes of relation of the three persons."[33]

Second, the understanding of God as both the immanent and the transcendent one is expressed in the Hebrew "I am who I am" *('ehyeh 'asher 'ehyeh)* and its abbreviated form "I AM" *('ehyeh);* both phrases are closely related to the Tetragrammaton (YHWH), the most holy and personal name of God. All three names seem to have derived from *hyh* ("be" or "being"), which can be translated as "to be," "to become," or even "is-ness." The verb *hyh* is the first person "qal" imperfect, connoting continuing action or reality. According to A. T. van Leeuwen, "The name Yahweh, which is in origin Kenite or Ugaritic, takes us back to an indefinable power encountered in the lightning and thunder."[34] The verb *hayah*, when it refers to God, "expresses his personal, dynamic, active being vis-à-vis his people and his creation."[35] In other

---

30. C. Kavin Rowe, "Luke and the Trinity: An Essay in Ecclesial Biblical Theology," *Scottish Journal of Theology* 56 (2003): 4: "the creeds can serve as hermeneutical guidelines to reading the Bible because it is in fact the biblical text itself that necessitated the creedal formulations."

31. See the excellent chapter on the Holy Spirit and the Trinity by Steven M. Studebaker, *From Pentecost to the Triune God* (Grand Rapids: Eerdmans, 2012), pp. 53-100.

32. Francis Watson, *Text, Church, and World: Biblical Interpretation in Theological Perspective* (Edinburgh: T&T Clark, 1994), pp. 140-45.

33. Holmes, *Quest for the Trinity*, p. 48 (emphasis mine).

34. A. T. van Leeuwen, *Christianity in World History*, trans. H. H. Hoskins (New York: Charles Scribner's Sons, 1964), p. 48. Just like another name of God, *El* or *Elohim* expresses "life in its power" or means "to be strong," "to be mighty" (Alan Richardson, *A Theological Word Book of the Bible* [New York: Macmillan, 1950], p. 91).

35. Van Leeuwen, *Christianity in World History*, p. 47; Durham, *Exodus*, 39; and Thor-

words, when "is" or "am" is used in Hebrew, its *verbal* significance is stressed. When "is" is used to refer to God, most English translations correctly render it as "came to" or "happened."[36] Thus "Yahweh" means "I make to be, whatever comes to be" in a causative sense,[37] marking God as the Wholly Other *and* Wholly Immanent, a God in relationship with the world and history. The context of the Exodus 3 passage also suggests God's doings. Verses 6, 15, and 16 emphatically declare God to be the God of the past, of Abraham, Isaac, and Jacob, who acted for them. God relates to the world in creation, preservation, direction, redemption.

Yet the Bible of the early church, the Septuagint (Greek Old Testament), translates the Hebrew verb "I am [who I am]" into a Greek participle functioning as a noun, "I am the being" *(egō eimi ho ōn),* thus providing the basis for Philo, as well as Origen and other church fathers, to perceive God essentially as Being. Is the Septuagint a mistranslation? Is the Hebrew Bible more authoritative than the Greek Bible? My answer is that it takes at least two languages to understand God, whose doing *and* being are in unity, and thus to perceive God more fully as the immanent-transcendent one. A Hebrew understanding must cross over its linguistic presuppositions and learn from the Greek the name of God, which embraces his "is-ness" or "being" as a nonsymbolic, ineffable, primordial concept or "pure being/substance."[38] Likewise, the Greek understanding must go beyond its philosophical assumption and learn from the Hebrew "I AM" and YHWH as a dynamic, active, living God who continuously acts in and interacts with his people and creation. This to me is the beginning of ecumenical theology. One should not bow to the god of logic (speculation), for one should only bow to the relational God of logic.

---

leif Boman, *Hebrew Thought Compared with Greek,* trans. Jules L. Moreau (Philadelphia: Westminster, 1960), p. 47: "The *hayah* of God is to act as God, to deal as God, and to carry into effect as God. . . . Continuously he shows himself in manifestation of grace and mighty acts as the God of Israel."

36. See Isa. 55:11, "so shall my word be," which goes on to state what it will do.

37. "With reference to the Lord the verb is used when he *does* something, when he *acts*" (Andrio König, *Here Am I* [Grand Rapids: Eerdmans, 1982], p. 67 [emphasis mine]).

38. Similarly, the "Wholly Other" terminology used by Karl Barth, Søren Kierkegaard, and Rudolf Otto; see Otto's *The Idea of the Holy: An Inquiry into the Nonrational Factor in the Idea of the Divine and Its Relation to the Rational,* trans. J. W. Harvey (Oxford: Oxford University Press, 1950).

The essays that follow raise a series of questions: How should non-Western Christians name God? Why are Allah, *Shang-ti,* and *Shin* appropriate, but Zeus and Buddha are not? Is Moltmann's understanding of a crucified God a modern form of patripassianism, that is, God the Father suffered on the cross and therefore changes in his divine nature? As the conversation in this volume will show, taking Scriptures, Christian traditions, and the contexts of the Christians seriously will provide a generative hermeneutics regarding how we name and understand God. This project works hard to invite Majority World readers to construct a theology, such as naming God, via a creative dialogue — using criteria such as that of Natee Tanchanpongs (biblical authenticity and his notion of moving toward Scriptures and context of readers), as well as the three patterns of naming the persons of the Trinity advocated by Kendall Soulen:[39]

1. A theological pattern that identifies the three persons in terms of the giving, receiving, and glorification of the divine name, the unspoken and untranslatable Tetragrammaton (YHWH) — referred to obliquely (the name, the LORD) or as a divine passive ("Blessed are . . . be comforted" in the beatitudes in Matthew 5, or "I am raised up" in Matt. 26:32).
2. A christological pattern that identifies the three persons as the Father, the Son, and the Holy Spirit. This pattern is relatively fixed in that it revolves chiefly around a limited set of male kinship terms (Father, Son, Spirit).
3. A pneumatological pattern that identifies the three persons by using an open-ended variety of ternaries (variables of three), such as "love, Lover, Beloved" (1 John 4:8, 16) or "God, Word, Breathe." And here we can add more contextual ternaries: "Root-Tree-Fruit, Sun-Ray-Apex, Fountain-River-Stream" (Tertullian); "Archetype, Image, Purifying Sun" (Basil the Great); "Revealer, Revelation, and Revealed-ness" (Barth, influenced by German idealism of absolute subject); "Primordial Being, Expressive Being, and Unitive Being" (John Macquarrie), *"Dao, De, Qi"* (Paul S. Chung, influenced by Daoist cosmology); "Mother Sophia, Jesus Sophia, Spirit Sophia" (Elizabeth Johnson, influenced by biblical feminism).

---

39. Soulen, *Distinguishing the Voices,* p. 22. See also Sallie McFague, *Models of God: Theology for an Ecological, Nuclear Age* (Philadelphia: Fortress, 1987).

It is our theological task to look for contextual and appropriate imagery to portray the mysterious, paradoxical nature of the Trinity, who is always in relation to and in interaction with the world. The content of the New Testament gospel message, expressed in narrative with multiple and spontaneous symbolic expressions of the mysterious God, can be translated into an ontological metaphysics. But one would want to avoid using highly abstract ontological terms to refer to the Trinity, making God into a static, aloof, and uncaring God. Most Majority World scholars in this volume lean toward the immanent and social aspects of the Trinity (following perhaps Moltmann's social trinitarian understanding based on the ancient doctrine of *perichoresis,* although classically the doctrine refers to the depth of the ontological identity of Father, Son, and Spirit!). They raise a critical question: Is ontology about the nature of a pure/essential substance (Bray says no)? Or is it about a personal existence that is relational at its base? The answer will determine for us whether freedom is a property of the person *(hypostasis)* or of the substance *(ousia).*[40] I find Karl Barth's dialectic understanding of the totally other God who makes himself known in Jesus Christ to be persuasive, and his strong thesis that "the One who loves in freedom" is necessarily triune.[41]

Conclusion

We are always at risk of projecting our minds and images onto God, even though we profess that God creates us in his image. This is what the third commandment (Exod. 20:7) warns against – not to take the name of God in vain – even as we are mandated and gifted to name him. Despite the risk of erring, devotion to God requires that we be faithful, for "the doctrine of the Trinity is basically an attempt to bring together the *incredible richness of the Christian understanding of God.* It is the distillation of the kaleidoscopic Christian experience of God in the light of its scriptural foundations."[42] The

40. See John D. Zizioulas (Greek Orthodox) following the Cappadocian fathers (e.g., St. Basil) on connecting being with personhood and relationality in his *Being as Communion: Studies in Personhood and the Church* (London: Darton, Longman & Todd, 1985).

41. Barth, *Church Dogmatics,* 1/1, p. 322.

42. Alister McGrath, *Understanding the Trinity* (Grand Rapids: Zondervan, 1988), p. 116 (emphasis mine).

hope and courage of our faith comes from the reality of the triune God himself. We witness from the gospel narrative the moment when "the innermost life of the Trinity is at stake." That is when "the Father suffers the death of the Son . . . and when in his descent into hell the Son loses the Father. . . . the Father loses the Son."[43] It is significant that the quest for the fuller reality of the Trinity is read in light of the Easter event. Thiselton writes of the power of the post-Easter triune God: "The Easter witnesses saw 'the glory of God in the face of Jesus Christ' (2 Cor. 4:6), as Jesus appeared in the likeness of God (2 Cor. 4:4), and as 'the reflection of God's glory and the exact imprint of God's very being' (Heb. 1:3). This raising takes place through the agency and activity of the Holy Spirit (Rom. 1:4; 8:11; 1 Pet. 3:18)."[44] In other words, the eternal love of the triune God has touched our historical process, so that although we often oscillate between tritheism and modalism, we can trust that God-in-Christ through the power of the Spirit will enable our myriad namings of God to embrace the fuller reality of the triune God — even as we are known by him (1 Cor. 8:3; cf. Gal. 4:9).

We often contemplate, as Job queries, "Can we know the deep [and beautiful/glorious] things of God?" (11:7) No *(via negativa) and* yes (through Christ) — "No one knows the Father except the Son" (Matt. 11:27). Through the person and event of Christ with the agency of the Holy Spirit, "God's being [and doing] is thinkable again,"[45] so that we can view ourselves and the world through God's eyes. Sitting at a round-table with our brothers and sisters from "every tribe and language and people and nation" (Rev. 5:9; 7:9; 13:7; 14:6) in a mansion with many windows will grant us a kaleidoscopic lens of the Easter reality — over and over again — as the biblical matrix patterns for us, the creedal affirmations guide us, and our contexts/horizons ground us in a more comprehensive view of the Trinity. Just as Paul's theology leads him to doxology, our knees will bend toward the earth and our songs rise to the heaven: "O the depth of the riches and wisdom and knowledge of [the Triune] God!" (Rom. 11:33-34)

43. Moltmann, *The Trinity and the Kingdom of God*, p. 81.

44. Thiselton, *Hermeneutics of Doctrine*, pp. 458-59.

45. Eberhard Jüngel, *God as the Mystery of the World* (Grand Rapids: Eerdmans, 1983), p. 111, taken from Thiselton, *Hermeneutics of Doctrine*, p. 474.

Postscript

The editors wish to express our heartfelt gratitude to the following partners in ministry for generously encouraging and sacrificially supporting this project: Michael Thomson at Wm. B. Eerdmans Publishing Company, Shen Li and Moses Cui in Beijing, the SEED Research Institute, the Earle M. and Virginia M. Combs Foundation, ScholarLeaders International, and the Rivendell Steward's Trust.

CHAPTER 1

One God in Trinity and Trinity in Unity

GERALD BRAY

ABSTRACT

The doctrine of the Trinity is fundamental to Christian faith. It has frequently been challenged, both inside and outside the church, but it has never been dislodged from its central position. The language used to explain it was developed in the early centuries of the church against the backdrop of Greek philosophy and Roman law, but it was not decisively shaped by them. On the contrary, Christians forged a new perception out of existing terminology and used it to impose their doctrine of God on what was to become the Western world. Since the sixteenth century that synthesis has been challenged, and more recently it has been dismissed altogether by Enlightenment and post-Enlightenment thinkers, but it continues to be defended by able Christian thinkers and remains a productive source of new thought. Today the church has to absorb that heritage and apply it in Majority World contexts, where the intellectual history of the doctrine may be unfamiliar. New expressions of it may have to be found, but the substance of the traditional teaching must not be lost or diminished in the process.

I. The Christian Doctrine of God

Few people would dispute that the doctrine of the Trinity is fundamental to the Christian faith. Even those who think it ought to be reformulated recognize that it lies at the heart of our prayers, hymns, and blessings. Jesus himself, just before he ascended into heaven, gave his disciples the Great Commission, to go into the whole world preaching the gospel and baptizing the nations in the name of the Father, the Son, and the Holy Spirit (Matt. 28:19). The Great Commission is a reminder to us that from the very beginning the three persons of the Godhead have been part of the church's message to the whole world.[1] The word "Trinity" may not have been used to describe it in New Testament times, but the idea was there and it has always been characteristic of Christianity. It was unknown to Judaism and as yet untested among (non-Jewish) Gentiles – a unique understanding of the one God that continues to challenge the church today as we seek to express it in our ongoing mission to new generations and cultures.

It may be true that the early church separated from Judaism more because it was prepared to admit Gentile believers without expecting them to become Jews first than because of its trinitarian beliefs about God. As far as we can tell, the Jewish opponents of Paul and the other apostles did not accuse them of preaching that there were three gods instead of one, though their claim that Jesus was the Messiah who had come down from heaven was clearly unacceptable to them.[2] The divinity of Christ was a doctrine that Jews could not accept, but Christians seem to have escaped the charge of tritheism because they always insisted that he was a revelation of the one God of the Bible, not a second deity that had appeared on earth. Much the same must be said for Christian teaching about the Holy Spirit. He was divine, but he was not a third god, a belief that might have been easier for Jews to accept because they did not distinguish him as a person. The Old Testament is full of references to "the Spirit of God," which are usually understood to be no more than a particular way of speaking about him, and as long as there was no formulated doctrine of the Trinity, Christian references to him could probably have been interpreted in that light.

Christians have always claimed to be monotheists – believers in one God, and for the most part Jews and Muslims have allowed that claim, even though they have both rejected the doctrine of the Trinity on the

1. See A. W. Wainwright, *The Trinity in the New Testament* (London: SPCK, 1962); and J. N. D. Kelly, *Early Christian Doctrines*, 5th ed. (London: Black, 1977), pp. 83-137, 252-79, for a comprehensive presentation of the evidence.

2. This is an obscure and highly contested subject. For a recent treatment, see Leo Duprée Sandgren, *Vines Intertwined: A History of Jews and Christians from the Babylonian Exile to the Advent of Islam* (Peabody, Mass.: Hendrickson, 2010).

ground that it is incompatible with true monotheism.[3] From their point of view, Christianity is inconsistent or mistaken in the way it honors Jesus Christ as God and regards the divine Spirit as a third divine person. To their minds, Jesus was no more than an extraordinarily gifted prophet and teacher, and the Holy Spirit can only be a particular characteristic of God that is frequently used to describe him. In response to this, Christians have traditionally replied that it is their experience of God that has forced them to develop a trinitarian understanding of him and that to abandon that understanding is to abandon the message of Christ himself. This is not to say that the church has never felt a need to seek theological reconciliation with the other great monotheistic religions. In our modern and increasingly globalized world there is considerable pressure on the three religions of Abraham, as they are often called, to patch up their differences and live in harmony.

According to one way of thinking that has been popular since the eighteenth-century Enlightenment in Europe, Jews, Christians, and Muslims all have their own understanding of God, but they all worship the same God, and so they ought to be able to accept one another as brothers and sisters in a common religious enterprise. That view did not get very far at the time, but it has come into its own in recent years, partly because of the horrors of the Holocaust and partly because of the rise of militant fundamentalism and continuing conflicts in the Middle East. These things have added a sense of urgency to the appeal that the great faiths should stand together, if not actually unite. Christians are now in danger of appearing to be the odd ones out because they cling to a doctrine of God that adherents of the other two faiths find unacceptable. Given that Christians claim to be monotheists, is the Trinity not an unnecessary complication that can and should be sidelined in the interests of peace and harmony?

It must be said that there are some within the Christian fold who are more than a little sympathetic to this plea. Such people may incline to the view that the Trinity developed against a backdrop of ancient Greek philosophy that has fundamentally distorted the faith and ought to be abandoned as a matter of principle, and not just as a diplomatic gesture in the direction of other monotheists. Surely it must be possible, they would argue, to honor Christ and speak of the

---

3. For a full discussion of the issues involved, see G. Emery and P. Gisel, *Le christianisme est-il un monothéisme?* (Geneva: Labor et Fides, 2001).

Holy Spirit without having to say that they are divine in the same way that God the Father is. They point out that there were many in the early church who regarded the Father of Jesus Christ as God in the Old Testament sense and who sought to interpret Jesus and the Holy Spirit as manifestations of him that were not separate persons in their own right. Can we not go back to that time and recover a supposedly "lost" Christianity that might bring us closer to our Jewish and Muslim colleagues?[4]

This theme, or variations of it, is common among liberal Christians, who often find it relatively easier to make common cause with similarly liberal Jews and Muslims than any of these do with more conservative followers of their own religion. Yet at the same time, there has been a remarkable revival of interest in the doctrine of the Trinity in Western theology, so much so, in fact, that it is now almost impossible to write a book on any theological subject without exploring its trinitarian dimension in the process.[5] Much of that is a fad and is overdone, but that does not matter. What is important is that the Trinity has become a benchmark for modern Christian theology so that whatever is said about other doctrines must take it into account and show how it relates to our understanding of every aspect of the Christian message.[6]

These two tendencies — the pressure for movement toward a generic monotheism and the revival of trinitarian teaching — coexist in the modern church, and so far nobody seems to have noticed that they are mutually incompatible, perhaps because their proponents move in different circles. Those who emphasize the commonality of the religions of Abraham often prioritize interfaith dialogue and are likely to include

4. On this subject, see Stephen Holmes, *The Quest for the Trinity: The Doctrine of God in Scripture, History and Modernity* (Downers Grove, Ill.: IVP Academic, 2012). For the challenge to traditional theism presented by process theology, see Bruce G. Epperly, *Process Theology: A Guide for the Perplexed* (London: T&T Clark, 2011); John B. Cobb Jr. and Clark H. Pinnock, *Searching for an Adequate God: A Dialogue between Process and Free Will Theists* (Grand Rapids: Eerdmans, 2000).

5. Much of this recent revival has been influenced by such works as Colin E. Gunton, *The Promise of Trinitarian Theology* (Edinburgh: T&T Clark, 1991), and T. F. Torrance, *The Trinitarian Faith* (Edinburgh: T&T Clark, 1988).

6. See Paul M. Collins, *The Trinity: A Guide for the Perplexed* (London: T&T Clark, 2008). For a wide-ranging exposition of the different views held on the subject at the present time, see Robert J. Wozniak and Giulio Maspero, *Rethinking Trinitarian Theology: Disputed Questions and Contemporary Issues in Trinitarian Theology* (London: T&T Clark, 2012).

a significant number of lay Christians who have little knowledge of, or time for, what they regard as theological subtleties like the Trinity. In contrast, those who find the Trinity everywhere in Christian teaching are more likely to be theologians with an investment in systematizing their own subdisciplines around a common theme. Dialogue with other faiths is unlikely to be very high on their agenda, if it figures at all. But in a global world, this inconsistency cannot continue forever. Sooner or later there will be conflict, and it is not unreasonable to suppose that it will erupt with particular force in the Majority World, where young Christians are confronted with a need to deepen their own faith and at the same time deal with the ever-present challenge of militant Islam. People in that situation cannot afford the luxury of academic religious dialogue. They have to give a reason for the hope that is within them, and be prepared to suffer for it at the hands of people who are determined to stamp out their witness. It is not enough to say that Muslim fundamentalists are a tiny minority even in their own cultures. That is true, but as Christians in many Islamic countries can testify, they are a hyperactive minority that is capable of doing great harm, not least to them. They certainly cannot be dismissed as an eccentric irrelevance in the way that similar Christian groups can be.

Christians in the Majority World are thus faced with a series of questions about the doctrine of the Trinity that they must answer if they are to survive and prosper. The first and most basic of these is straightforward – do we need the Trinity at all? Can we not express our belief in God, Christ, and the Spirit in some simpler way that will avoid giving offense to other monotheists? How important is the traditional doctrine of the Trinity for expressing our Christian convictions? Can we safely leave it to one side as a complicated problem that the ordinary person does not need to bother with? Can it be reconstructed in a way that would help to indigenize it in recently Christianized cultures, making it seem less of a Western import and more attuned to the thoughts and needs of new believers? Or is the doctrine of the Trinity so totally bound up with ancient Greek thought that if the latter is discarded it would collapse of its own accord? In other words, can it be expressed in other thought forms, or is it just the product of a tradition that was once dominant but that is now being challenged and may soon lose its remaining influence in the Christian world?

At this point we should perhaps stand back from particular contexts and consider how far the challenge of trinitarian doctrine is common to the entire Christian world. In the West it takes particular forms that on the surface may appear to be alien in many parts of the Majority World, but we should not be misled by this. The problems we face go right back to the beginnings of the Christian faith, before there was a West or a Majority World in the modern sense. Christians have always had to explain a belief that on the surface makes no sense and appears to be unnecessarily complicated. Had it been to their advantage not to construct such a doctrine it is hard to believe that they would have done it in defiance of their own best interests. It flies in the face not only of Judaism but of the Greek philosophical tradition as well.[7] If the Jews could not conceive of any plurality in God, the Greeks could not think of the supreme being in personal terms. To them, ultimate reality was an idea, not a person with whom they could have an interactive relationship. It is true that their gods were personal, rather in the way that Hindu gods are, but that merely emphasized the fact that they were not absolute, and therefore not what the Jews meant by God at all. To be personal was to be relational, but in the Greek mind to be relational was to be relative — none of their personal gods could claim to be the one true Being in himself.

For the Christian church faced with these challenges, the basic questions were the same then as they are now. What lies at the heart of the universe? How can we relate to that reality, if indeed we can? The gospel message was that God, the ultimate Being, had revealed himself to the world in Jesus Christ and continues to do so in and through his Holy Spirit. This was the context in which Christians sought to answer these questions, and the result was the doctrine of the Trinity. Whatever we do with that doctrine today, the same questions confront us as Christians in the modern world, whether we accept the Western tradition as normative for the whole church or seek to replace it with something that we think is more attuned to our own needs and circumstances.

II. The Traditional Doctrine

Before we examine what possibilities there might be for revising the traditional doctrine of the Trinity, we have to understand what that

---

7. For this development, see R. P. C. Hanson, *The Search for the Christian Doctrine of God* (Edinburgh: T&T Clark, 1988).

is and how it came into being. The detailed history has often been recounted elsewhere, and there is neither the time nor the need for us to cover the ground again. But if we are thinking of building anew, we have to understand what building blocks were felt to be necessary for the construction of the traditional doctrine and why they were pieced together in the way they were. We must also appreciate that there were a number of other possible constructs, some of which were very appealing to large numbers of early Christians, but that in the end they were all found to be inadequate for one reason or another. What we have inherited has stood the test of time and surpassed the claims of its rivals, and so it must be taken seriously, even if we think there may be reasons for thinking it can (or must) be reformulated in the modern theological and missional context.

The first principle of traditional Western trinitarianism is that God is one. Whatever else we say about him, we cannot allow the fundamental unity of his divine being to be compromised. The second principle is that the Father, the Son, and the Holy Spirit coexist within that divine being.[8] They are not different names for the same objective being, because they interact with one another and there are some things that only one of them has done, like become a man in Jesus Christ. We are therefore forced to insist on their distinctiveness, however we choose to describe it. Whether they are equal to one another is more difficult to determine. As part of God's being they must be the same, since God's being is one, but in their relationships to each other they reveal a pattern in which the Father appears to be somehow greater than either the Son or the Spirit. How the Son and the Holy Spirit are related to each other is much less clear and has been the subject of an ongoing and still unresolved controversy, but they are not interchangeable. Furthermore, there is an order among them that allows the Father to send the Son into the world, but not the other way round, and that also allows the Holy Spirit to take the Son's place in the life of the church without repeating his atoning sacrifice on the cross. To what extent their different functions reflect a fundamental difference that is inherent in their identities is one of the most enduring questions of trinitarian theology. Have the persons acted as they have by their own free choice, or is there something in who they are that predetermined how they would act?

8. See G. L. Prestige, *God in Patristic Thought*, 2nd ed. (London: SPCK, 1952).

The early Christians tackled this question by starting with the assumption that the one God could be equated with the Father. When Jesus told his disciples to pray to God as their Father, they could hardly have imagined that the Father could have been anyone other than the God of Abraham, Isaac, and Jacob, in whom they already believed. What Jesus was teaching them was to look at him in a new way.[9] Just as his God was their God, so his Father would be their Father too. That basic assumption led the first generations of the church to think of the Son and the Spirit as extensions of the Father, but they soon found themselves in trouble with that analysis. For example, they could say that the Son was the mind of the Father, but not that the Father lost his mind when the Son became a man. They could also imagine that Father, Son, and Holy Spirit were distinguished by their functions, so that the Father was the Creator, the Son was the Redeemer, and the Holy Spirit was the Sanctifier. That sounded better, but in the end it did not work very well because the New Testament tells us that the Son was also the Creator (John 1:3; Col. 1:15-16), the Father was the Redeemer (John 3:16), and both the Father and the Son are sanctifiers. Separation according to function did not work, nor could it, since it is hard to see how redemption can be distinguished from sanctification in the new creation. What the members of the Godhead do, they do together.

The end result of these attempts to account for the threeness in God was to reinforce the supremacy of the Father and downgrade the divinity of the Son. The Holy Spirit was seldom mentioned at this early stage, but we can probably assume that if the Son was regarded as being less than fully God the same would also have been true of the Spirit. By the time the church emerged from the shadows of persecution into the daylight of legality, the various options that had been canvassed for the previous 250 years were fading into the background. In their place, however, came the greatest challenge of all — the heresy we now know as Arianism. How much Arianism had to do with Arius, the Alexandrian presbyter after whom it is named, and whether it can really be seen as a single belief system, are questions we can leave to the historians.[10] For our present purposes, the problem was that the

9. This is fully explained in Gerald L. Bray, *God Has Spoken* (Wheaton: Crossway, 2014).

10. See, e.g., Rowan Williams, *Arius: Heresy and Tradition* (London: Darton, Longman and Todd, 1987); Michele René Barnes and D. H. Williams, eds., *Arianism after Arius: Essays on the Development of the Fourth-century Trinitarian Conflicts* (Edinburgh: T&T

Arians denied the divinity of the Son and insisted that he was no more than the greatest of the creatures. It is true that they thought he had been created in heaven before the foundation of the world, and that he was closer to God the Father than any angel was, but despite his lofty status, he was still not God.

Arianism owed its popularity to its simplicity. There is only one God, that God is the Father, so the Son is by definition not God, even if he is as close to divinity as it is possible for a creature to be. Its opponents argued that between the Creator and the creation there is a great gulf fixed — if the Son was a creature, then not only was he not God but he could not be our Savior or Mediator either. As a creature he had no special standing with the Creator, and if he became sin for us, as the New Testament says he did, then he became a sinner and had no authority to save us from our transgressions. The crisis that Arianism produced led to the First Council of Nicaea in 325, where a serious attempt was made to sort out the terminology used to describe the Son.

The fathers of Nicaea recognized that the Son has his own identity, quite distinct from that of the Father, but they insisted that he was fully and properly God at the same time. To describe him, they said that he was "consubstantial" with the Father, meaning by this that his being was the same as that of the Father. The main problem they faced was that the Greek word for "consubstantial" *(homoousios)* was not in the New Testament but had apparently been used by third-century heretics who wanted to say that the Son was the Father in another form, or "mode" of being. That would have destroyed his distinct identity because he would have been no more than a façade behind which the Father was to be found hiding, a heresy we now know as modalism or Sabellianism, after the man who is supposed to have advocated it. It was true, of course, that Jesus had told his disciples that he and the Father were one, but whatever that meant, it did not mean that he was merely the Father in disguise. The New Testament evidence presents us with two subjects who are in conscious dialogue with one another, and that had to be accounted for. The modalist approach would have meant that when Jesus prayed to his Father he was either talking to himself or he was a man talking to God in the Arian sense of a creature speaking to the Creator.

Clark, 1993). There is also a lengthy exposition in Aloys Grillmeier, *Christ in Christian Tradition*, trans. John Bowden, 2nd ed. (London: Mowbray, 1975), 1:219-328.

Neither of these options was adequate. By adopting the word "consubstantial," the First Council of Nicaea sought to establish parameters within which the debate must proceed, but it could not produce a definitive solution to the problem raised by confessing the divinity of the Son. Their failure in this respect became obvious in the following generation. Granted that we must say the Son is consubstantial with the Father, in what sense is this true? Human beings are consubstantial with one another — we share the same kind of being and nature, we can copulate and reproduce, we can even share blood and body parts to a limited degree. This is possible because we are like one another without being exactly the same, and it was natural for some people to want to interpret the Father, Son, and Holy Spirit in an analogous way. The snag was that while human beings exist in plurality, there is only one God. Father, Son, and Holy Spirit are not related to each other like Tom, Dick, and Harry — three separate beings sharing the same analogous nature. Rather, they are three distinct identities sharing the same being, and for this a new terminology had to be found.

In searching for the right words to use, the early church found it relatively easy to agree about how to describe the oneness of God. This was his being or substance and his nature, which were one and the same.[11] For example, God was good, but he was fully and absolutely good, and so Father, Son, and Holy Spirit were each fully and absolutely good too. Here the logic of monotheism is plain to see, and at this level the early Christian understanding of God is scarcely different from either the Jewish or the Muslim one.

It was much harder for the church to find a word to describe the threeness in that one divine being. The two most successful terms were the Greek *hypostasis* and the Latin *persona. Hypostasis* can be found in the New Testament, in Hebrews 1:3, where the Son is described as the "*character* of the Father's *hypostasis*," whatever that is supposed to mean. There has been considerable debate about this over the years, but the context suggests that the best translation is something like "the exact replica of the Father's identity." A *character* was a copy or a stamp, hence the idea of "replica," while a *hypostasis* was an underlying reality. The snag was that the word was often used as a synonym for "being," and in its Latin form, *substantia*, that is what it came to mean

---

11. On this concept and its relationship to Greek philosophy in particular, see Christopher Stead, *Divine Substance* (Oxford: Clarendon, 1977).

more or less exclusively. Thus while Greeks could and did say that there were three *hypostases* in the one being of God, the Latins could not translate this as "three substances in the one substance."

To get around this problem Tertullian came up with the word *persona*, which had originally meant a mask in the theatre but had come to signify an agent in a lawsuit as well. A *persona* was someone who could act in a court of law, a dimension that was missing from the word *hypostasis*.[12] The difference can be seen in that whereas *hypostasis* was not confined to human beings, since animals and inanimate objects can also have an identity, *persona* more or less was. I say "more or less" because in Roman law not every human being was a legal *persona* – women, children, and slaves were all excluded – and it was possible for a business entity to acquire legal personality, or as we would say today, to be "incorporated," which simply means "to be given a body."

Whether the word *persona* occurs in the Bible or not is hard to say. Its Greek equivalent *prosōpon* certainly does, especially in the phrase *prosōpon pros prosōpon*, which is the standard translation of the Hebrew for "face to face." Its most famous occurrence in the New Testament is in 1 Corinthians 13:12, where Paul says that though we now see through a glass darkly, we shall then see "face to face." The mystery will be unveiled, and we shall know God just as he knows us. What is particularly interesting is that in this passage, *prosōpon* cannot possibly mean mask because it is explicitly used to describe the exact opposite. For Paul, to see God "face to face" is to be unmasked; it is, in effect, what we could now quite happily refer to as "person-to-person" contact. In other words, Paul's use of the word *prosōpon* is closer to what we now understand as "person" than it is to the original meaning of "mask," and it is on that basis that the early Christians took it over for theological purposes.

In finding this word Tertullian struck it rich, as we might say today. It enabled him to say that in God there were three persons in one substance – the same formula that we continue to use now. He may not have understood it in precisely the way that we do, but his terminology was sufficiently flexible that it could adapt to later theological

12. The fullest discussion of this is in R. Braun, *Deus Christianorum: Recherches sur le vocabulaire doctrinal de Tertullien*, 2nd ed. (Paris: Etudes Augustiniennes, 1977), pp. 207-42. For a more recent and wide-ranging treatment of the word "person," see B. Meunier, *La personne et le christianisme ancien* (Paris: Cerf, 2006).

developments and survive without change. The Greek world hesitated over this for a long time, preferring the formula "three *hypostases* in one being" but occasionally flirting with *prosōpon* as an alternative. The question was finally resolved at the Council of Chalcedon in 451, where it was decreed that *hypostasis* and *prosōpon* were synonymous and could be used interchangeably. In practice, what that meant was that the word *hypostasis* was redefined so as to accord with the Latin *persona*, which also became the model for understanding *prosōpon*.

The details are complex, but the underlying principles are clear enough. What the Chalcedonian Definition achieved was a balance between two different levels of perception that can be traced back to a number of Greek thinkers of the late fourth century but that was not formally canonized until the council.[13] Chalcedon got to that point by making a clear distinction between the level of particular identities in God, where there were three persons, and the level of his being, which was only one. Previously it had usually been imagined that the one somehow expanded into three or that the three coalesced into the one, but by positing two different levels of analysis, Chalcedon was able to avoid this. In its understanding, which in many ways reflects that of the great Cappadocian fathers of the late fourth century, the one did not become three or the three one. Instead, the three were simultaneously present in the one and the one in the three and there was no crossover from one level to the other. In other words, the Father could no longer be seen as God in the true or absolute sense in a way that did not apply equally to the Son and the Holy Spirit, because although the last two depended on the Father with respect to their personal identities, they did not do so in regard to their common being, in which they all shared equally. The Father might personify the mysterious being of God to a degree that the Son and the Holy Spirit did not, but if so, that was because he remained eternally transcendent in heaven and not because he was innately superior to the other two persons.

Just as importantly, though this is not always properly recognized, the Chalcedonian Definition of faith gave priority to the three persons of the Godhead over their one being or nature. It envisaged a God whose three persons possess their one nature and are free to use it to shape their common divine will. This conclusion was imposed on them by the incarnation of the Son, because in that act he took on a

13. On Chalcedon, see R. V. Sellers, *The Council of Chalcedon* (London: SPCK, 1961).

second, human nature while remaining the divine person, with his divine nature, that he was in eternity. The fact that he could do this, without involving the Father and the Holy Spirit in the same process, showed that as a divine person the Son was not bound by his divine nature but was able to transcend it and become a man, not by diminishing his divinity but by adding to it. It took several more centuries to work out the finer points of this doctrine, but the essential framework was laid at Chalcedon and that has remained the standard formulation of trinitarian doctrine ever since. There were dissenters at Chalcedon who refused to sign on to its Christology, but even they accepted the trinitarian aspect of the decisions taken there, so that all Christians now confess that God is three persons in one being or substance and interpret these terms in basically the same way.

III. Reconstructing the Doctrine

What was decided at Chalcedon and the councils that later clarified its definition has remained the official orthodoxy of most of the Eastern and all of the Western churches from then until now. It was questioned from time to time, especially after the rise of Islam, and during the Middle Ages it was elaborated by a number of philosophical theologians who sought to integrate the doctrine of the Trinity into their systematization of truth. To a man like Richard of St. Victor in the twelfth century, the Trinity was not only a revealed doctrine but also an essential part of created reality, reflected in any number of analogies that were readily available to those who used their minds to think about them and could be used to explain the underlying structure of the universe.[14] It was not until the sixteenth century, when Renaissance humanists uncovered vast tracts of ancient philosophy and science that had either been lost or forgotten, and when the Protestant Reformers called into question the biblical foundations of the church's teaching, that serious attempts were made to overturn it on the ground that it was a philosophical construct and not part of God's revelation at all.

---

14. Richard has been rediscovered recently in the English-speaking world. See, e.g., Ruben Angelici, *Richard of Saint Victor: On the Trinity* (Eugene, Ore.: Cascade, 2011) and Boyd Taylor Coolman and Dale M. Coulter, *Trinity and Creation* (Hyde Park, N.Y.: New City Press, 2011), pp. 195-352.

The most important of these attempts to undo the Trinity was something close to what we now call Unitarianism, though that doctrine emerged independently in the early eighteenth century. We meet it in the pages of Calvin's *Institutes* (1.13), where the great Reformer had to deal with unnamed men who were attacking the legitimacy of the traditional theological terminology. In the early seventeenth century this way of thinking was generally associated with Socinianism, a doctrine derived from the teaching of Lelio Sozzini and his nephew Fausto, two Italian lawyers who propagated it.[15] Socinianism was regarded as a great danger in the early seventeenth century, but although it was largely snuffed out, at least in Western Europe, it left an abiding legacy. Its principle that theological doctrine should always be susceptible to rational analysis was attractive to many and became a commonplace even among some theologians, like the famous Hugo Grotius, who dissented from the Sozzini and argued against them. Three persons in one divine being did not make logical sense, and so the doctrine of the Trinity was living on borrowed time in a world that was increasingly governed by the power of reason.

Eighteenth-century Unitarianism was a kind of upgraded Socinianism in which the antitrinitarian element, as its name indicates, was unmistakable. It was never accepted as orthodox teaching by any Christian church, and to this day Unitarians are not officially recognized as Christians, but their impact has been far greater than such rejection and denial might suggest. For although no church has ever adopted Unitarian beliefs outright, many of their leading theologians have shared the mindset that produced it and have taught a theoretically "orthodox" form of Christianity that for all intents and purposes is indistinguishable from Unitarianism. The doctrine of the Trinity has been progressively sidelined in Western seminaries to the point where few pastors and even fewer laypeople know what to say about it. Worse still, they do not think that the Trinity is very important. They believe that they can preach and teach the gospel on the basis of the Bible without indulging in such theological abstractions and find it hard to see why anyone should challenge them in this belief. They do not ig-

---

15. On Socinianism, see Philip Dixon, *Nice and Hot Disputes: The Doctrine of the Trinity in the Seventeenth Century* (London: T&T Clark, 2003); Sarah Mortimer, *Reason and Religion in the English Revolution: The Challenge of Socinianism* (Cambridge: Cambridge University Press, 2010).

nore Jesus Christ, who remains central to their perception of God's revelation to the world, and many of them pay great attention to the Holy Spirit. What they find difficult is linking them together as three equal persons in one God, but that, of course, is what the doctrine of the Trinity is all about.

It is essential to understand that the antitrinitarianism of the past five centuries has been the outward and visible sign of a progressive but often covert secularization in Western society. Belief in miracles, superstitions of various kinds, and reliance on divine revelation as opposed to human reason have all been dismissed as relics of a medieval past. The concept of God has occasionally survived in the form of a "supreme being," "intelligent designer," or "first principle" that holds the universe together, but whether there really is such a thing is debated, and if there is, whether it ought to be equated with the Christian God is regarded as a matter of personal opinion.[16] Christians will tend to do that, either from conviction or tradition, and others will not, but to the liberal mind that does not matter very much. As long as people recognize that there is something out there that is bigger than themselves, we can get along by calling it different things and relating to it in different ways. However we approach it though, the Trinity is an irrelevance, either because it is a mistaken formulation held over from a bygone era by the weight and inertia of traditional orthodoxy or because it is an irretrievably Western picture of God. This, by and large, is where the West and its theologians are coming from today, though by no means all of them have succumbed to this logic. On the contrary, there has been a major trinitarian revival in the late twentieth century, which started against that background and must be seen in that light, but has headed off in quite a different direction.

When we turn to the Majority World, the theological picture is more complex. The influence of Western secularism is certainly widespread, especially in those countries that have come under Communist rule at some stage, but not only there. The governing elites have

---

16. It is significant that the defenders of "intelligent design" in the United States have insisted that theirs is not a religiously based theory but one that can be justified on scientific principles alone. Equally significant is the fact that the courts have generally disagreed with them when the matter has been put to adjudication. For a discussion of modern theism that does not involve trinitarian belief, see David J. Bartholomew, *God, Chance and Purpose. Can God Have it Both Ways?* (Cambridge: Cambridge University Press, 2008).

almost all been educated in Western universities and have absorbed their philosophy to a greater or lesser degree. As a result, in most cases local universities and other centers of learning act as secularist embassies in what is intellectually a foreign country to them. The grassroots church, however, appears very different. In Western countries, secularization has taken hold of a large proportion of the population. Some people remain religious, and a great many are privately superstitious, but for the most part such things are kept out of the public domain. Religion has become a private matter left to the individual conscience, which in practice means that God cannot be mentioned in public discourse in any serious way. This is true even in theological faculties, where the methods of debate and research parallel those used in every other academic discipline. Belief in God can be studied as a social phenomenon, but it cannot be used as the basis for constructing policy. Here we have gone well beyond any form of Unitarianism into outright atheism, where the Christian doctrine of the Trinity has no logical place.

In the Majority World, by contrast, spirituality is the stuff of everyday life. Whether people believe in spirits, pagan gods, or some higher form of religion, the whole of life is permeated with a sense of the presence of the divine. What Christianity has done, especially in Africa, has been to structure that instinctive awareness in a systematic way that appeals to history, philosophy, and personal experience. What was previously mysterious, disordered, or threatening has become clear, orderly, and positive. At this level, it must be recognized that Islam has performed a similar function in the places where it has gone, and it is here that the potential for conflict between the two great religions arises. Christian systematization of the spiritual world includes a doctrine of the Trinity, but its Islamic equivalent does not. More importantly, Islam does not simply ignore the Trinity – it excludes it. Where the prevailing culture is still animist or polytheist, a different problem arises. People there may have little trouble understanding that there are three divine persons, but why should there be only three? And how does that affect our understanding and experience of God, who can surely be called by many names without detracting from his supreme sovereignty. In these contexts, the church faces a different battle, though in a curious way, the two worlds can overlap at the academic level. Liberal theologians who call for a restructuring of the Christian doctrine of God to take account of modern perceptions of reality may sound very much like, and even make common cause with, representatives of the conservative Majority World who want to explain God in terms that are meaningful to their own people. For different reasons, both types of people find traditional orthodoxy hard to swallow, and there is a very real possibility that the Western liberals will deconstruct Christian doctrine in a way that will appeal to Majority World thinkers who want to appear to be sophisticated and who will be attracted by the apparent simplicity and practicality of what amounts to Unitarianism. Why learn a complex theological formula when a simple "love God and your neighbor" will apparently do instead?

How can we deal with these challenges, and in what way can the West and the Majority World work together? First of all, Western theologians need to recognize that most of the criticisms leveled against traditional trinitarian doctrine, which have to do with the supposedly inappropriate use of the terms "person" and "substance" in the way we define it, are misguided. The charge made against "substance" is that it is an outdated scientific concept. It has been abandoned in physics, the argument goes, so it should be abandoned in metaphysics as well. The root of the problem here is philosophical, not theological. There has always been a complex and difficult relationship between these two disciplines, but theologians must point out that the biblical revelation has never been captive to any secular philosophy. It does not need the word "substance" to describe God, who is there whatever term we use. In fact, there is a long tradition of Christian thought that has rejected the use of words like "substance" and "being" to describe God precisely because he cannot be pinned down in this way. To define him in terms derived from natural science is to make an intellectual idol of him. That may be more sophisticated than statues of gold and silver, but it is just as inaccurate and unacceptable. Whatever we say about God in human language, it is only an approximate and therefore inadequate description of him.

At the same time, we must insist that God is really there, that he has a presence that cannot be denied, and that he is fundamental to our existence. In much Western thought, the abandonment of terms like "substance" has led, not to a deeper theological understanding, but to atheism, and it is this that we must do all in our power to avoid. For this reason, we probably cannot abandon the vocabulary of "substance" as long as there is no alternative readily available, but we can certainly reassure our critics that we are not wedded to it as a matter of principle. Come up with something better and we shall be only too willing to adopt it.

Where "person" is concerned, the main objection is that in modern secular usage the term refers to a "center of consciousness" that is supposed to be the unique possession of each individual. But there cannot be three centers of consciousness in God, because if there were, there would be three different gods and not one. This argument is appealing at first sight, but it is flawed. First of all, to assert that a person is a center of consciousness raises doubts about the status of human beings who, for one reason or another, are not conscious. We cannot explore this theme in detail here, but suffice it to say that Christian opposition to abortion and euthanasia is rooted in the belief that a person cannot be defined in that way. The Christian hope in life after death is also bound up with this – an inert corpse is not the end of our life, but the sign that we have moved on to a higher reality. For Christians, to be a human person is to be created in the image and likeness of God, because God is personal. Even if we are not conscious, this is still true.

But equally important, and it is here that the West and the Majority World can perhaps most easily converge, to be a person is to exist in relationships – with God primarily, but also with other human beings. It is often said nowadays that the West is too individualistic, whereas the Majority World places a much higher value on the importance of community. How true this really is is hard to say. It seems probable that the Majority World is moving in the direction of greater individualism, and there are signs that the West is rediscovering the importance of community.[17] Be that as it may, there is no doubt that both worlds are built on a structure of relationships, however they are defined. The persons of the Trinity are the ultimate example of this – the absolute relationships into which believers are integrated by being united with Christ in the power of the Holy Spirit. This is true whoever we are, wherever we come from, and whatever intellectual or cultural formation we have had. The rediscovery of this principle in Western theology has given new life to the doctrine of the Trinity, which is now interpreted much more in the context of interpersonal

---

17. See, e.g., Alan J. Torrance, *Persons in Communion: Trinitarian Description and Human Participation* (Edinburgh: T&T Clark, 1996).

relationships than it ever used to be. This is perhaps the most encouraging sign that theological renewal in the West is possible and that it can connect with the concerns and experience of the Majority World at the deepest level.

The Christian doctrine of the Trinity is that God is love, and that he manifests himself to us as a community in which his love is perfected. Love is not a substance, not a thing that can be objectified and defined, but it is a reality and constitutes the being of God. Those who live in love are the persons of the Trinity, and it is as persons created in God's image that we are invited to share in their eternal fellowship. We cannot exclude the possibility that this reality might be expressed in other ways, and perhaps one day new doctrinal definitions will be found that can describe it as well or better than what has been achieved in the past. But whatever the future holds in this respect, it is certain that nothing that does not contain and enhance this reality will ever take the place of traditional trinitarian doctrine, nor is it likely that this truth will be expressed in one cultural context to the exclusion of others. Jesus commissioned his followers to make disciples of all the nations, baptizing them in the name of the Father, the Son, and the Holy Spirit. Over the centuries the church has proclaimed this message not so much by adapting to the prevailing cultural norms as by transforming them into something higher, which only divine revelation is capable of expressing adequately. Let us pray that as our mission enters a new phase this conviction and this awareness will continue to guide us and that we may be led into all truth as we believe our forefathers in the faith were.

Further Reading

Philip M. Collins, *The Trinity: A Guide for the Perplexed* (London: T&T Clark, 2008).

Colin E. Gunton, *The Promise of Trinitarian Theology* (Edinburgh: T&T Clark, 1991).

Stephen Holmes, *The Quest for the Trinity* (Downers Grove, Ill.: IVP Academic, 2012).

T. F. Torrance, *The Trinitarian Faith* (Edinburgh: T&T Clark, 1988).

Robert J. Wozniak and Giulio Maspero, *Rethinking Trinitarian Theology* (London: T&T Clark, 2012).

CHAPTER 2

Beyond Homoiousios *and* Homoousios:
Exploring North American Indigenous Concepts
of the Shalom Community of God[1]

RANDY S. WOODLEY

ABSTRACT

The fourth-century battle over the interpretation of a single developed trinitarian theology laid the groundwork for numerous binary trajectories, with some resulting in Christian imperialism. Western Christianity's early preoccupation with divine ontology, coupled with the military might of the Christian empire and the West's inability to hold the mystery of God in tension, has beleaguered Christians and other monotheists for centuries. An Indigenous understanding of the divine shalom community may offer different choices that are perhaps closer to the constructed understandings of Trinity held by early followers of the Christ. In their various perceptions, early Jewish Christians recognized and acknowledged a place in their worldview for a trinitarian construct without the trappings of extrinsic categorization or the bur-

1. Shalom, as used in Scripture, is a very broad theological construct. I am using it according to Walter Brueggemann's model, which he describes as follows: "That persistent vision of joy, well-being, harmony and prosperity is not captured in any single word or idea in the Bible; a cluster of words is required to express its many dimensions and subtle nuances: love, loyalty, truth, grace, salvation, justice, blessings, righteousness. But the term that in recent discussions has been used to summarize that controlling vision is *shalom*. Both in such discussion and in the Bible itself, it bears tremendous freight — the freight of a dream of God that resists all our tendencies to division, hostility, fear, drivenness, and misery. *Shalom* is the substance of the biblical vision of one community embracing all creation. It refers to all those resources and factors that make communal harmony joyous and effective." Walter Brueggemann, *Peace: Living Toward a Vision* (St. Louis: Chalice, 2001), p. 14.

(funny, we think of it as 'hello')

37

den of ontological fixation. If we must talk of God in ontological terms, which again is beyond any of our comprehension, then perhaps the image of the community of the Creator, existing eternally in shalom relationality, can lead us beyond much of the former dialogue that has centered itself on ontological substance, and toward a better understanding of our own communal ontology.

Introduction

There is no way for us today to gauge the perceptual difficulties early Jewish followers of Jesus went through when moving from a monotheistic construct of God to a trinitarian construct. From what we can garner from the writings of the New Testament, it is apparent that the divinity of Jesus struck them with such intensity that an alternative view of the divine was impending and necessary.[2] Therefore, it is paramount in discussing Jesus' divinity to acknowledge that according to several writers in the New Testament, Jesus is recognized as the divine Creator. The literary structure of New Testament references to Christ as Creator are predominately in formulaic style, meaning they may have been mnemonic devices memorized as poems or sung as hymns. These formulaic patterns suggest that the early Jewish understanding of Christ as Creator somehow equated Jesus with YHWH and that it was a popular theme in the early church. Here is the account found in the Gospel of John.

> In the beginning was the Word, and the Word was with God, and the Word was God.
> He was in the beginning with God.
> All things came into being through him, and without him not one thing came into being. What has come into being in him was life, and the life was the light of all people. (John 1:1-4 NRSV)

In the writer's mind, Jesus is preexistent, divine, was God's instrument in creation, and gave life to all creation. In the same

---

2. The Gospels and much of Paul's writings are largely a defense of Christ's divinity without the direct assertion that Christ himself understood his purpose to be more than that of the expected Jewish Messiah.

chapter, verses 10-14, the writer speaks of God's redemptive value in Christ. The writer seems to have a fluid understanding of Jesus the man and Jesus the preexistent Christ who is Creator. The writer of John also appears to understand the very same Jesus as the redeemer of all things. In a similar formulaic pattern to the one found in John, Paul writes,

> He is the image of the invisible God, the firstborn of all creation;
> for in him all things in heaven and on earth were created, things visible and invisible, whether thrones or dominions or rulers or powers – all things have been created through him and for him.
> He himself is before all things, and in him all things hold together.
> He is the head of the body, the church; he is the beginning, the firstborn from the dead, so that he might come to have first place in everything.
> For in him all the fullness of God was pleased to dwell, and through him God was pleased to reconcile to himself all things, whether on earth or in heaven, by making peace through the blood of his cross. (Col. 1:15-20 NRSV)

In this text Paul understands:

- Christ as preexistent
- Christ as having supremacy over all creation
- Christ as God's instrument in creation
- All creation as being created by Christ
- All creation made for Christ
- Christ making shalom with all creation by his redemptive atonement.

Paul's explanation parallels John's understanding of Christ the human, Christ the Creator, and Christ the Redeemer. Paul references another formulaic description of Christ as Creator in 1 Corinthians 8:6: "Yet for us there is one God, the Father, from whom are all things and for whom we exist, and one Lord, Jesus Christ, through whom are all things and through whom we exist" (NRSV). Once again, Paul states that through Jesus Christ, God made all creation, and through Christ we all have life.

A fourth reference, possibly constructed in a similar kind of formula, is found in the Letter to the Hebrews:

> Long ago God spoke to our ancestors in many and various ways by the prophets, but in these last days he has spoken to us by a Son, whom he appointed heir of all things, through whom he also created the worlds. (Heb. 1:1-2 NRSV)

As with the other passages, the writer of Hebrews begins by reasoning that, through Christ, God created all of creation and that all creation belongs to him. Later, the same writer (Heb. 2:10) ties the creation act to Christ's redemptive actions by saying, "It was fitting that God, for whom and through whom all things exist, in bringing many children to glory, should make the pioneer of their salvation perfect through sufferings" (NRSV).

In this great mystery of incarnation and reconciliation, those who walked with or near the incarnated Christ came to an understanding that he was the orchestrator of creation. Without a better understanding of God's plan through Jesus Christ as both Creator and as Savior/Reconciler (shalom-bringer), we in the modern church may have over-zealously developed an imbalanced salvation theology that favors the otherworldly over our physical realities. Among traditional Indigenous peoples, God inhabits all creation. God is in every tree, every rock, and every stream.[3]

---

3. The idea of physical *place* should not be overlooked when referencing the Trinity. As a settler-colonial society, the West has placed an emphasis on *time* to the deprecation of serious thinking concerning *place*. The emphasis of time over place naturally bends Christianity toward an abstract trajectory to the point where systematic theology and practical theology become two distinct realities. The author understands that it is difficult to form a righteous theology of place when the historical reality begins from a place of stolen land, but as a result, in a Western worldview Trinity is a very abstract or even ethereal ideal. Among Indigenous peoples, when thinking about the trinitarian community, *place* can take on relational aspects that are neglected by an emphasis on time.

Many traditional Native Americans would understand the nature of God in regard to creation to be panentheistic. Pantheism, on the one hand, is the belief that the created order *is* God and God *is* the created order. Panentheism, on the other hand, is a constructed word from the Greek meaning "all-in-God," with the distinction that, while the world and universe are contained within God, God is greater than the whole of the universe and creation. From this position there can be significant variation on

[handwritten marginalia:] Time & place are connected in hame o yeshua

The Creator of all things is also the reconciler of all things, and all things (i.e., all creation) are being created for Christ. Paul, in the Colossians passage, even says Christ "holds all things together." It may be said that since all things are redeemable in Christ, then restoring the world to God's intentions of shalom is the point of Christ's redemption. The basic issue in our day is perhaps the breadth of healing God has made available in Christ. If Jesus died for all creation, and not just the human "soul," and not even just for humans (all things), then the concept of redemption is much broader than many Christians have traditionally thought. Redemption (our salvation) is reconciliation of and for the whole earth.

Part of the problem contributing to a limited view of salvation is Western Christianity's insistence on binary choices (i.e., divine/human, created/not created, Creator/Redeemer, Father/Son), which may be compounded in both the English language and Western logic. For example, in the Cherokee language we are able to use a phrase that points to Jesus as the *Creator-Son*. This linguistic construction references Jesus' sonship in relation to the Father while at the same time referencing his role in creation. The word "son" in Cherokee is related to the word for egg. An egg is both chicken and egg at the same time.[4] The respected Keetoowah Cherokee tradition keeper Thomas Belt, in an essay coauthored with Margaret Bender, says concerning the Cherokee word for egg,

> In Cherokee, one's child is *agwe'tsi*, "my egg." The child is inseparable from the speaker in two ways: first, a possessive pronoun is built into the word as a prefix (in this case in the form *agw-*, "my") so that

---

how the relationship between God and creation plays out. Also, as stated, the fingerprint of God or DNA is on all creation, allowing trinitarian concepts to become tangible and accessible. For a detailed philosophical article on panentheism, see John Culp, "Panentheism," in *Stanford Encyclopedia of Philosophy*, ed. Edward N. Zalta, spring 2013 ed., http://plato.stanford.edu/entries/panentheism/. For a more complete historical theology, see Sean M. McDonough, *Christ as Creator: Origins of a New Testament Doctrine* (Oxford: Oxford University Press, 2009).

4. I first heard the term "Creator-Son" used in 2001 by fellow Cherokee theologian Robert Francis, who later told me he had earlier heard me use it in a song. I use the term "Creator-Son" to designate "Creator" as Jesus' relationship to the Trinity and the efficacy of his role in the whole creation process. The use of the term "Son" refers to Jesus' *kenosis* as the member of the Trinity who became the "Son of Man" on earth. As I will explain, this idea is inherent in the Cherokee language.

no child is an abstraction but is always the child of a specific person in a conversation; second, a child's biological origin as a part of the parent is reinforced throughout life since the word for child also means "egg."[5]

When used with the word for Creator, the Son becomes connected to the Creator through relationship and becomes indistinguishable from that relationship. In this simple linguistic formula Jesus is acknowledged as both divine Creator and divine Son. The implications of embracing broader understandings of Christ as the one who creates all things and as the one who restores all things has tremendous significance for the *missio Dei* as well as theological import.[6] The God who creates all creation also sends, is sent to, and will restore all creation. Jesus, the Creator-Son, is one in indistinguishable relationship with God, sent by God, to redeem all things to God. This brings us back to the problem of the modern West and the dilemma the title of this essay alludes to; is Jesus the same as or similar to God?

I. Giving One Iota

The early church, in defending Christ's divinity against various heresies, primarily Arianism (the Son is the first and highest creation of the Father), Ebionism (the Son is only apparently divine), and Docetism (the Son is only apparently human), created a quandary for trinitarians and nontrinitarians alike. How can Christians, after investing in centuries of persecuting one another for various trinitarian positions surrounding Christ, move beyond the ontology of trinitarian *personae*?

One of the earliest controversies in Christianity focused on Jesus Christ, the Son, in the trinitarian construct. The two Greek words rep-

5. Thomas Belt and Margaret Bender, "Speaking Difference to Power: The Importance of Linguistic Sovereignty," in *Foundations of First Peoples' Sovereignty: History, Education and Culture*, ed. Ulrike Wiethaus (New York: Peter Lang, 2008), p. 189.

6. Given the fact that *shalom* has never been used as a model for mission among Native Americans, the relationality of the Trinity could serve as a vital missional model in this process. Since the widespread understanding of *shalom* is found among almost all North American Indians, there is an immediate common point of reference between Native American symbols, stories, and ceremonies that promote harmony and what the Bible presents as God's vision of *shalom*.

resenting one significant dispute were *homoiousios*, "of a similar substance," and *homoousios*, "of the same substance." It has been pointed out many times that these two words differ by a single letter, *iota*, the smallest in the Greek alphabet.

I would like to suggest in this essay (even while attempting to convey my own ontological understanding) that we can move beyond traditional arguments concerning the ontology of God. The ontological question of the Trinity is one we may *ask* but not one over which we should *divide* ourselves. Ontological notions of God require proof beyond what any human can produce, so ultimately our understanding of God's ontological essence may be simply a matter of our best understandings and faith.[7] We Christians accept the construct of a monotheistic faith. As evangelicals we accept the inclusion of Jesus and Spirit as in eternal relationship with God. In terms of how we pray (and avoiding modalism) we believe in faith that God hears us, yet the full answer to who God is remains a great mystery. Without certainty of proof, we must admit that the great mystery is just that – a mystery to us.

II. A Different Way of Thinking

There may be room in the "Native American Old Testament"[8] for renewed trinitarian constructs; especially given the similarities between Native American views and those of *shalom* as developed in Judaism.[9] Similar to the early Jewish Christian monotheistic com-

7. I often use a phrase in my courses, "there is no such thing as theology, there are only theologies." When humans attempt to articulate their understandings and experiences of the divine, those descriptions become inseparably bound to ourselves and to our own experiences, which give formation to the language we have available to comprehend. All our explanations inevitably assume a sense of anthropomorphism.

8. See Steve Charleston's essay, "The Old Testament of Native America," in *Native and Christian: Indigenous Voices on Religious Identity in the United States and Canada*, ed. James Treat (New York: Routledge, 1996), which helps deepen our understanding of these two ancient covenants. Charleston avers, "God spoke to generations of Native People over centuries of our spiritual development. We need to pay attention to that voice, to be respectful of the covenant" (p. 69).

9. The sources confirming the commonly held principles of harmony among Native Americans are many and varied in nuance, but it can be stated without great disputation that most North American Indigenous tribes held to a lifeway of harmony. In general, the list of tribes whose overriding lifeway/philosophy promotes harmony

munity, Native Americans are able to look back from the vantage point of history to understand God as a great mystery or even a divine trinitarian mystery. Although rare, some pre-European-invasion Indigenous Native North American sects even held a trinitarian view of the Creator. Aboriginal North Americans are not dependent on Western church history, church councils, and doctrinal development in order to validate their views of trinitarian plausibility. Reexamining Native American views of God in light of past trinitarian revelation may provide new light from an alternative worldview, which could lead to a deeper understanding of the divine mystery and the earthly *shalom* community.

Indigenous peoples do not think about theology in the same categories as Westerners.[10] Only within the last several decades have Native American Christians begun to do significant work on compiling, writing, and sharing their understanding of Christian theology. Many factors help explain why this is the case, but primarily, Native Americans have not been encouraged to share their perspectives in Western-dominated Christian theological circles. Particular to the subject at hand is not that Indigenous peoples are not thinking about concepts like Trinity, but rather they are struggling to find ways to communicate their insights in ways that are true to their culture and worldviews.

Indigenous North American cultural understandings, worldviews, and ways of disseminating knowledge are drastically different from Western paradigms and are often diametrically opposed to them. Further complicating things is the problem that not only are the categories incompatible with Indigenous thinking, but there is also currently no existing model or construct for translating traditional

---

could include almost every North American Native tribal group. The similarities between God's vision of *shalom* and what Native Americans view as the Harmony Way are incontrovertible. There are many innate aspects in Native American cultures that promote biblical *shalom*, or what we as First Nations call *shalom* by other names. For a more thorough understanding of the intersection of the Native American Harmony Way and Walter Brueggemann's construct of *shalom*, see my "The Harmony Way: Integrating Indigenous Values within Native North American Theology and Mission" (Ph.d. diss., Asbury Theological Seminary, 2010).

10. For example, consider the North American Institute for Indigenous Theological Studies (NAIITS), which is one example of how Indigenous theological dialogue is changing. For information on NAIITS please see the website at: http://www.naiits.com/.

Native beliefs into Western Christian theology. Indigenous theologians who wish to discuss such topics are at a disadvantage with few choices available.

The choice most often taken by the Indigenous theologian is assimilative, learning all the histories and categories of the West, even though to many Indigenous theologians they seem anemic and separate from the whole of reality. Another alternative (and these are not mutually exclusive choices) is to simply begin by sitting down and asking other Indigenous thinkers the question, "What do our elders, spiritual leaders, and other traditional people say about this theological concept?" Since the answer to that question will typically be, "nothing directly," Indigenous scholars can begin exploring what aspects of their traditional beliefs carry the same concepts or fit within the same paradigms as the Christian beliefs they are seeking to understand.[11]

While Native North Americans do have room in their worldview for Trinity, and sometimes even with direct historic evidence of a trinitarian understanding of God, this understanding has been overlooked because of categorical differences. These categorical differences, the result of a Western paradigm for approaching theological study, are directly traced back to Greek systems of thought, having influenced Western thinkers how to extrinsically categorize and dissect concepts, and define objects by their attributes and separate them accordingly. This type of thinking has been the dominating influence in Western doctrinal development. Aboriginal Americans have no such major in-

---

11. It should not be surprising that there are few direct parallels between Native American theological beliefs and modern theological Christian constructs. This does not mean that there are no opportunities for crossover between them or that traditional Native beliefs are incompatible with Christian theological concepts. In fact, many Indigenous Christian thinkers would argue that there is a great amount of support for Christian beliefs in traditional Native religious understandings. For example, there have been strong parallels drawn between traditional Native beliefs and the Jewish concept of *shalom* theology (Woodley, "Harmony Way"). This is not an unfounded opinion. It has been pointed out that much of the Jewish Old Testament theology omits significant aspects of the Christian faith — the Trinity, for example — and yet still is seen as supportive of the Christian faith. In regard to the Old Testament, the more "ancient" religious traditions are reinterpreted and filtered through the lens of our later understandings and given new meaning. This is what many Indigenous followers of Jesus are attempting to do with their traditional Native beliefs.

fluence. Because of this, America's First Nations have their own way of understanding the relational independence, interdependence, and connectivity of the trinitarian mystery.

Native American views of God are defined almost completely by relationality rather than by function.[12] In other words, the different aspects of the Trinity are not determined by their function so much as by how they relate in community.[13] Recent theological discussions are focusing more on sacred community/*perichoresis*[14] in developing an understanding that the ontology of the Trinity is not to be found in the persons but rather in the relationship (Zizioulas, Barth, Moltmann, Boff, Grenz, Olson). In terms of common dialogue potential with First Nations theologians, this is a positive change from the usual Western form. Non-Western thinkers tend to be able to hold two seemingly opposite views in tension with little problem. The theological difficulty for Native Americans may come when discussing the independent aspects of the Trinity rather than relational interconnectivity.[15] Recent

12. The relationality of the Christian Trinity as community becomes all-important for Indigenous peoples. The pre-Enlightenment worldviews of the writers of the New Testament have a great affinity with non-Western/communal Indigenous-oriented thinking, such as is found among Native North Americans. Since we see little writing about the Trinity (proper) in Scripture, one interpretation may be that the church of the New Testament was able to hold the tension of the "three-in-one" with less difficulty than the later, Greek-influenced theologians who would follow them.

13. A word should be said about parallels concerning First Nations constructs of the Sacred Spirit and the Holy Spirit ("holy" is a synonym for "sacred"). The Spirit is recognized as a continual working of God upon the earth and is the source of life as well as our connection to God. It is God's Spirit working on earth that is the all-encompassing manifestation of God's presence here. In this sense, and because of the length of this essay, suffice it to say that the way Western thinkers frame the Spirit is similar to the way Native people do. The Spirit functions in everything and in everyday life as God's presence. The primary difference would be the Indigenous thought concerning God's active presence in all creation. In other words, nothing is inanimate to the Indigenous mind.

14. Early Christian uses of the term have been ascribed to church leaders such as Gregory of Nazianzus, Hilary of Poitiers, Athanasius, Maximus the Confessor, Gregory of Nyssa, and John of Damascus. Regardless of their different understandings and usages, the point I am making is that the concept of *perichoresis* was marginalized by the Western church until recently.

15. Ironically, this would seem to be the opposite of the issue that Western theologians have. An example of this kind of categorization would be the church split between the Western and Eastern churches in the eleventh century. At its heart, the

46

postmodern theological discussions also promise meaningful dialogue with Indigenous peoples.[16]

III. Indigenous North American Trinitarian Concepts

Because early European settler-colonial literature is so sparse concerning the subject at hand, we only have the records of a few eyewitnesses to rely on concerning early Indigenous American constructs of the divine Trinity. Among Cherokee scholars there is general acknowledgment of an ancient trinitarianism, but it is based on little written record or deep traditional knowledge. A trinity of creator beings is found in the oral traditions among the Cherokee and several other tribes. One of these references is an account by a writer in the 1930s describing an ancient Cherokee concept of a Supreme Trinity. The writer records, "Much like our Trinity, they were called *Uhahetaqua,* the Supreme Power, and *Atanati* and *Usquahula.* Although they were three distinct beings they were always unanimous in thought and action."[17]

A second reference hints at the ontological unity of purpose of the Cherokee Trinity:

> The other "sect," with far fewer followers, believed that there were only three beings above, "always together and of the same mind," who sit in three white seats and receive all prayers and determine when each person must die. Such interpretations were strengthened by the recognition that those who held to the three primordial beings were apparently well versed in traditional Cherokee religion.[18]

issue revolved around the *filioque* controversy, which was a debate about the categories of the trinitarian figures and their roles in regard to each other independently.

16. Olson, Grenz, Boff, and even Moltmann might be considered viable candidates, but in particular I am referring to Austin J. Roberts, *Perichoresis and Process: The Eco-theologies of Jürgen Moltmann and John Cobb* (Claremont, Calif.: Imago Futura, 2012).

17. Hugh T. Cunningham, "A History of the Cherokee Indians," *Chronicles of Oklahoma* 8, no. 3 (September 1930): 291, http://digital.library.okstate.edu/Chronicles/v008/v008p291.html.

18. Lee Irwin, "Museum of the Cherokee Indian in Cooperation with The Cherokee Historical Association and Western Carolina University Different Voices Together: Preservation and Acculturation in Early 19th Century Cherokee Religion," *Journal of Cherokee Studies* 18 (1997): 12.

A fascinating trinitarian account in colonial Native American encounters comes from the journals of John Wesley. The following excerpt, from Wesley's 1736 journal, reflects his experience among another southeastern Indian tribe, the Chickasaw Indians:

> Tues. 20 [July] — Five of the Chicasaw Indians (twenty of whom had been in Savannah several days) came to see us, with Mr. Andrews, their interpreter. They were all warriors, four of them head men. The two chief were Paustoobee and Mingo Mattaw. Our conference was as follows:
>
> Q. Do you believe there is One above who is over all things? Paustoobee answered,
>
> A. We believe there are four beloved things above; the clouds, the sun, the clear sky, and He that lives in the clear sky.
>
> Q. Do you believe that there is but One that lives in the clear sky?
>
> A. We believe there are two with him, three in all.[19]

Further in his journal, after clarifying that this Native traditional belief is in reference to the one God, and not angels or spirit beings, Wesley simply moves on without further questions. It is unclear whether Wesley found it surprising that the Chickasaws had a trinitarian theology, or if he completely missed what they were saying, or perhaps he simply had no way of processing what they were describing.[20] However, it is obvious from his journal that such trinitarian beliefs were in fact held and espoused by traditional Natives.[21]

Some have argued that all Native American thinking concerning the Trinity was later adaptations of reports of the Christian Trinity. This position does not explain the fact that a trinity of creator beings

19. *The Works of John Wesley*, vol. 1, *Journals from October 14, 1735 to November 29, 1745*, 3rd ed. (Peabody, Mass.: Hendrickson, 1984), p. 37.

20. My opinion is that Wesley was unable to grasp the possibility of a Trinity construct among a people he considered to be pagan. Wesley's inability to compare trinitarian views was based on the typical bias of the era.

21. It should be mentioned here that though there are no particular distinctions made in these trinitarian traditions that represent a specific concept of the Holy Spirit in the Trinity, this should not be surprising. As we have discussed, such categorization would be completely foreign to a Native way of thinking. The essential aspect of these stories, however, is that they represent the concept of a three-in-one view of the Great Spirit that, though not generally held by all Native traditions, was at least an accepted construct among some.

is found in early Native American literature and in the oral traditions, particularly among the Cherokee. Early reports of Cherokee trinitarianism are recognized and confirmed by a variety of scholars, of whom perhaps the most prolific and respected in Cherokee literature is William G. McLoughlin. Says McLoughlin, "Myths, now lost, may have told of three superior beings that later myths call the 'Creators' or the 'Masters of Life' or 'Givers of Breath' who were responsible for giving life to human beings, but these myths have not survived except as we find them in the later 'fractured myths' of the early nineteenth century."[22] Again, McLoughlin leaves room for the authentic possibility of divine triune Cherokee Creators by stating, "Creation and genesis myths in this period [circa 1821] took many forms, indicating their popularity and the unsettled nature of Indian speculation about this question. They differed as to whether there was one, two or three creators at work."[23]

Another report from a southeastern Indian tribe from an earlier time period (circa 1728) concerns the Saponi, a Siouan tribe in Virginia, which confirms the plausibility of a Creator within a communal theistic structure. William Byrd explains what was reported to him by his Saponi guide, Bearskin:

> He told us he believed that there was one Supreme God, who had several Subaltern Deities under Him. And that this Master-God made the World a long time ago. That he told the Sun, the Moon, and Stars, their business in the Beginning, which they, with good looking after, have faithfully performed ever since. That the same Power that made all these things at first, has taken care to keep them in the same Method and Motion ever since.[24]

There are also nonsoutheastern Native American tribes who have theological constructs that appear to be trinitarian in some fashion. For example, Cree theologian Ray Aldred has suggested the possibility that the Cree worship a Supreme Being, yet with three manifestations

22. William G. McLoughlin, *The Cherokees and Christianity, 1794-1870: Essays on Acculturation and Cultural Persistence,* ed. Walter H. Conser Jr. (Athens: University of Georgia Press, 1994), p. 160.

23. McGloughlin, *The Cherokees and Christianity,* p. 163.

24. John R. Swanton, *The Indians of the Southeastern United States* (1946; Washington, D.C.: Smithsonian Institution Press, 1977), pp. 749-50.

of power, including Manitou, Thunderbird, and Bear.[25] The point here is that there is little angst and tension regarding such matters among American Indians.

IV. The Great Mystery as Three in One

I think neither Jesus nor the early church ever imagined a religion where orthodoxy was enforced by anyone, much less the state during and after the Constantinian era. In the Nicene Creed we find the first universal document representing orthodox Christianity influenced by the utopian legacies of the Greeks, in propositional form and in adherence to truthful knowledge rather than truthful moral character, along with Roman imperialism. Numerous examples in the Gospel writings lead readers to believe that Jesus would condemn rather than embrace the offspring of such a marriage (Matt. 21:28-32; Luke 4; Luke 10:29-37). Heterodoxy may or may not have been the norm in the Gospels, but the Christ who is presented in the Gospel accounts would certainly not pardon most forms of an enforced orthodoxy. Says respected elder and Seneca scholar John Mohawk,

> Once established, the institutions that represented the utopian vision of the Kingdom of God — the Roman and Greek churches — took steps to strengthen and fortify their control, particularly any deviation in matters of doctrine and belief. The survival strategies of institutions that inherit utopian legacies can become intensely repressive in nature, policing behavior and even thought in order to maintain their control. In the Christian establishment these strategies produced repression, excommunications, the search for heretics, the Inquisition, witchcraft trials, and the ruthless use of torture, executions, and even mass slaughter — all in the cause of advancing a religion that once claimed itself committed to the principles of peace.[26]

25. From a conversation with Ray Aldred (Cree) on April 25, 2005. I have chosen to focus this study on Trinity beliefs in the Southeast because of my familiarity with the literature. By doing this, I have resisted the temptation to interpolate and I have left room for others to explore their own tribal beliefs without undue influence as a result of my naïveté. I mention my conversation with Ray because he is familiar with both the culture and literature that put forth a Cree Trinity construct.

26. John Mohawk, *Utopian Legacies: A History of Conquest and Oppression in the Western World* (San Francisco: Clear Light, 2000), pp. 262-63.

References to American Indian historic trinitarian constructs of the deity are few and far between. Even I, a Cherokee scholar, feel somewhat apprehensive in discussing the mystery of the great mystery in such detail. Yet bridges need to be built in order to promote mutual understanding and respect between settler-colonial theologies and American Indigenous theologies. Osage scholar George Tinker, relying on the work of Seneca scholar Barbara Mann, effectively argues both for an American Indian reciprocal dualism and that God cannot be one.[27] Says Tinker,

> So first of all, the notion of a single creator immediately participates in the dysfunctionality of the number one, signaling a hierarchical order of creation. The dualistic opposite, rather than a feminine co-participant, is then abject evil, or the Devil, something entirely lacking in Indian cultures until it was read back into our traditions by missionaries who needed to find (and still do) an equivalent evil to fit their own theologies. For Indian folk, the notion of a single, male sky god is decisively unbalanced and leads to chaos, competition, male supremacy, racial hierarchy, and competing notions of a single (doctrinal?) truth over against falsehood, hearsay, and evil. It immediately allows for an anthropology that is decidedly anthropocentric and elevates the human (superior) over all other life-forms (the inferior), and equally allows for the elevation of male over female — since it is the male/man/*adam* who is particularly made in the image of the christian, male sky god.[28]

I believe (and my guess is that Tinker does as well) that American Indian theological divine premises are probably more varied, complex, and left to mystery than a complementary dualism, or as he calls it, "collateral-egalitarian image schema as community,"[29] would

---

27. This argument is made by Seneca scholar Barbara Mann, *Iroquoian Women: The Gantowisais* (New York: Peter Lang, 2000), p. 63, and Osage scholar George Tinker in his essay, "Why I Do Not Believe in a Creator," in *Buffalo Shout, Salmon Cry: Conversations on Creation, Land Justice, and Life Together,* ed. Steve Heinrichs (Waterloo, Ont.: Herald Press, 2013), pp. 171-72. While Tinker is attempting to make the point that the understanding of one Creator is a missionary construct perpetuated for convenience by colonized Native Americans, the same rationale for his argument can be used to explain that God is not one but three in one.

28. Tinker, "Why I Do Not Believe in a Creator," p. 172.

29. Tinker, "Why I Do Not Believe in a Creator," p. 172.

suggest. The brilliance of his argument is that a single, noncomplex divine ontology cannot exist in harmony with what we all see plainly in creation. However, it is easy to understand how any religion viewed through the imperial cultural lens of kings and kingdoms, especially those in which that religion is married to the state, will produce a hierarchical, single, high god-king.

Also, I would argue that the DNA of the Creator is primarily found in the witness of that which has been created, and nature is more complex than a theory based on dualities would suggest. I would like to propose that when we focus on the divine ontology our focus should primarily be on the communal aspects of God, nature, and human organizing.

When considering the dynamics of Trinity, if God does exist as *one in one* (an A alone model), then the lens of imperialism would be at least partially correct in believing God is something akin to a benevolent dictator. In such a model it would make sense that God orders all creation to act within certain reasonable parameters and human organization should reasonably follow in step with a hierarchical model of organization. In the God-as-one-in-one model, God's love is given to creation because of God's inherent wisdom as the Creator, and we become wise through giving the Creator our patronage and our worship. American settler-colonial organizing appears to reflect this understanding. The difficulty is that grasping how much this understanding forms and reflects our theology is likely impossible, though there does seem to be a relationship between the two. The problem with God as one in one is the incongruence with both nature and social relationships. Nothing of creation reflects such a simplistically individualistic model.

If the divine ontology is *two in one*, then perhaps the imagery of a perfect marriage is appropriate for the divine being. The divine couple, if you will, respond to one another in love and as an example, expecting all creation to do likewise. In a sense, God as *two in one* simply mirrors a double benevolent dictatorship of two who rule instead of one. In the A to B model, there are only three possibilities of relational dynamics, that is, A to B, B to A, and A together with B.

God as *three in one* presents the first possibility of matching the relational and ontological DNA found in all creation and human community. The basic building block of human life, all the way down to subatomic particles, is both simple and complex, containing a harmonious existence of unity and diversity.[30] Imagining the divine being as three in one is also the first opportunity to reveal God as community operating in deference and preference to one another as one interso-cial being. Rather than the limited relationship of only three possible permutations of the two-in-one model, the relational possibilities of God's ontology as three in one (A-B-C) become much more complex, presenting an extraordinary number of relational permutations. An A-B-C ontology is much closer to the makeup of all creation, as well as reflecting how we relate to one another in human community. In the trinitarian model, God is community, which may also reflect the divine sense of community in all creation; in other words, community is innate to, and created by, the community of the Creator.

An A-B-C imagery of the divine may include aspects or character-istics of the other two models, but it is infinitely more beautiful in its simplicity, and yet more complex than the alternatives. I understand the community-of-the-Creator model expressed in the Gospels con-cerning Jesus, whose actions and teachings surrounding human com-munity were a direct result of a shalom community ethic, based pri-marily through a harmonious, communal lens. Jesus' understanding of God's "kingdom" is a shalom community of egalitarianism, where peace reigns and the most marginalized in society are cared for.

Jesus spent his life forming community. He included the outcast and disenfranchised. Women, shepherds, lepers, tax gatherers, Gen-tiles, the infirm, and others who made up the marginalized of society formed his community. Jesus' teachings exemplified by parables such as those found in Luke 15 point directly to God's deepest desires being for community.[31] Other New Testament writings expound on the value of unity and diversity and egalitarian community as the norm of the church (1 Cor. 11–12; 1 Pet. 4:8-11). The image of God as community and as a model of community, I would argue, goes far deeper in our souls than that of the image of a God who is expecting community. If we must talk of God in ontological terms, which, again, is beyond any of our comprehension, then perhaps the image of the community of the Creator, existing eternally in shalom relationality, can lead us beyond

30. For the implications of unity and diversity in all creation and the Scriptures, see Randy Woodley, *Shalom and the Community of Creation: An Indigenous Vision* (Grand Rapids: Eerdmans, 2012), pp. 80-91, and my earlier book, *Living in Color: Embracing God's Plan For Ethnic Diversity* (Downers Grove, Ill.: InterVarsity Press, 2004).

31. See my exposition of Luke 15 in *Shalom and the Community of Creation*, pp. 80-91.

much of the former dialogue that has centered itself on ontological substance and toward a better understanding of our own communal ontology.

Further Reading

Leonardo Boff, *Trinity and Society* (reprint, Eugene, Ore.: Wipf & Stock, 2005).

Vine Deloria Jr., *God Is Red: A Native View of Religion* (Golden, Colo.: Fulcrum, 2003).

Stanley Grenz, *The Social God and the Relational Self* (Louisville: Westminster John Knox, 2001).

Veli-Matti Kärkkäinen, *The Trinity: Global Perspectives* (Louisville: Westminster John Knox, 2007).

Clara Sue Kidwell, Homer Noley, and George E. Tinker, *A Native American Theology* (Maryknoll, N.Y.: Orbis, 2003).

Jürgen Moltmann, *The Trinity and the Kingdom* (Minneapolis: Fortress, 1993).

Catherine Mowry LaCugna, *God for Us: The Trinity and Christian Life* (San Francisco: HarperSanFrancisco, 1993).

Karl Rahner, *The Trinity* (New York: Crossroad, 1997).

Richard Twiss, *Rescuing Theology from the Cowboys: An Emerging Indigenous Expression of the Jesus Way in North America* (forthcoming).

Miroslav Volf, *After Our Likeness: The Church as the Image of the Trinity* (Grand Rapids: Eerdmans, 1997).

Randy Woodley, *Shalom and the Community of Creation: An Indigenous Vision* (Grand Rapids: Eerdmans, 2012).

John Zizioulas, *Communion and Otherness: Further Studies in Personhood and the Church* (London: T&T Clark, 2007).

Also see all volumes of the *Journal of North American Institute for Indigenous Theological Studies* (Winnipeg).

CHAPTER 3

The Trinity in Africa: Trends and Trajectories

SAMUEL WAJE KUNHIYOP

ABSTRACT

God and the idea of the Trinity are no strange beliefs in Africa. The Supreme Being (God) is a commonly held belief among all African peoples, predating Christianity and Islam. Africa also played a formative role in the development of the concept of the Trinity. Tertullian, an African theologian, is credited with being the first theologian to coin the word "Trinity." The Ethiopian Orthodox Church is the only church in Africa that traces its trinitarian beliefs and practice to the fourth century. The thesis of this chapter is that though classical trinitarian belief is historically and biblically and theologically true, its presence in the contemporary African church is practically disregarded and absent. The church is recommended to go back and emphasize trinitarian theology in its theology and practice.

Introduction

Christians do not just believe in God; they affirm the real existence of three persons in the Godhead, namely God the Father, God the Son, and God the Holy Spirit. Obviously, this is not a simple and straightforward belief. This highly thought out and very complex concept has been in existence from the rise of Christianity to its present articulated position. The belief in the triune God is not just an abstract theological postulation by sophisticated theologians, but has serious meaning and implications for Christian spirituality and practice. Why is a study on the Trinity important? Harold O. J. Brown struck it well. "Without a coherent doctrine of the Trinity, the New Testament witness to the activity of God in Christ and in the work of the Holy Spirit will tend to force one either into modalism or a kind of tritheism."[1] In other words, one cannot ignore it and not fall into serious heresy of some sort.

Though, as I will argue, biblical Christianity cannot exist without trinitarian theology, sadly we find that Christianity as practiced in most of contemporary African Christianity either ignores, disregards, or simply does not appreciate its meaning and significance. This development is especially worrisome as the Pentecostal movement is attracting millions of members who are untaught and ignorant of key cardinal doctrines of the Christian church.

In some Christian circles, preachers make pronouncements such as "Don't expect to understand it, just believe or accept." The problem is that the statement is half true and half false. Yes, it is true that we cannot understand the Trinity fully, but this does not mean that we are unable to understand anything. Yes, it is a mystery, but it does not mean that God has not revealed anything about this concept and that we cannot say anything intellectually rational about it. This is a sad commentary on the church and should not be the case.

In this chapter, I will examine this doctrine not only from a historical and biblical perspective, but even more so from an African historical, cultural, and religious context. I will look critically at the Ethiopian Orthodox Church, the oldest form of Christianity in Africa, and how it has been able to continue emphasizing the Trinity as a cardinal aspect of its life and practice. This chapter will also survey both contemporary distortions of the Trinity in the African church and Islamic rejection of the Trinity. I will also provide a biblical summary of trinitarian theology, and note how it should influence spiritual life and practice.

I. African Concept of God

There is no gainsaying that Africans who come to the Christian faith already have a belief in the existence of God and the spirit world.

---

1. Harold O. J. Brown, *Heresies: The Image of Christ in the Mirror of Heresy and Orthodoxy from the Apostles to the Present* (Grand Rapids: Baker, 1988), p. 154.

Evidence for the African belief in God can be seen in the variety of names for God among all African peoples, as well as in religious beliefs and practices, rituals and sacrifices. God is viewed as supreme, all-powerful, all-knowing, loving, and caring. The most important and critical question is: Is the Supreme Being whom Africans acknowledge the same as the God of the Bible? John Mbiti, probably the most prominent and influential African theologian on this subject, considers this to be the case. So does Bolaji Idowu, who argues on the basis of general revelation that God has revealed himself to Africans and is worshiped by them.[2]

At most, the beliefs and practices of African Traditional Religion convey only a faint and incomplete understanding of who God is. For example, even if we grant the concept of the supreme God who is the same as the God of the Bible, we must ask, What about the concept of the triune God in African conceptions of God? Some African theologians have argued that the concept of the Trinity is present and well-articulated in the African understanding of God. A. Okechukwu Ogbonnaya, who opposes monotheism (Idowu) and polytheism as depictions of the African understanding of God, postulates:

> The Concept of the One is present in African religions, but so also is the concept of the Many. . . . The concept of the Divine as community actually does more justice to African conceptions of God. For this, we need another term, a word like communotheism; a community of gods. Community, in the African sense, will reflect better the affirmation of both the One and the Many than the categories of monotheism and polytheism. The noun communotheism communicates the idea that Divinity is communal.[3]

Ogbonnaya uses community theism from an African perspective to explore the Christian concept of the Trinity. What is unclear is the identity of the community gods. It is not explained who these community gods are. To his credit, there are great lessons to be learned about the relational aspect of the Godhead in terms of relationships

---

2. Bolaji Idowu, *Towards an Indigenous Church* (London: Oxford University Press, 1965), pp. 24-26.

3. A. Okechukwu Ogbonnaya, *On Communitarian Divinity: An African Interpretation of the Trinity* (St. Paul: Paragon, 1998), pp. 27-28.

between the persons. However, it must be pointed out that the image of the community of relationships between (among?) the gods in the African sense at best underscores the importance of relationships, but fails to deal with the equality in the Godhead that biblical Christianity affirms. The point is, relational and communal aspects of the Trinity are not the same as the metaphysical issues involved in the Trinity. This is a category mistake. For Ogbonnaya, the Trinity must be true because Africans so perceive it in their world. As I argued in *African Christian Theology*, seeking to justify and authenticate our theology from our own experience or from below has inherent weaknesses.[4] If the concept is true, it must be derived first from above or as revealed in his Word. Otherwise we end up with a doctrine that is our cultural conception. The Bible is the textbook for evaluating our doctrine, not our worldview or context, although we acknowledge that our worldview and context do influence our use and application of the Bible. Clearly, though there is a community of gods, the supreme God is ontologically not equal to the other gods. We also affirm the pervasive nature of the idea of community in Africa; without it one cannot fully understand the African worldview. The most severe criticism of communotheism or social theory is that of polytheism – a plurality of gods. A plurality of gods is closer to polytheism and tritheism, which both biblical revelation and historic, biblical Christianity see as heretical. Community among these many gods cannot be postulated as the best tool for understanding and stating trinitarian theology.

II. Trinity in African Christianity

The earliest contact between Africans and the idea of the Trinity goes back as early as the fourth century, when the Ethiopians were introduced to Christianity. History has it that "paganism and Judaism were practised side by side in Ethiopia before the introduction of Christianity."[5] In their pre-Jewish and pre-Christian religion, the Ethiopians were polytheistic, with temples, altars, and statues of gods all over the land.

4. Samuel Waje Kunhiyop, *African Christian Theology* (Grand Rapids: Zondervan, 2012), pp. 78-80.

5. Sergew Hable Selassie, "The Establishment of the Ethiopian Church," in *The Church of Ethiopia: A Panorama of History and Spiritual Life* (Addis Ababa: Ethiopian Orthodox Church, 1997), p. 1.

There is also biblical and historical evidence that Judaism was introduced into Ethiopia. The Bible tells of the story of the queen of Sheba of Ethiopia visiting King Solomon during his peak period as king of Israel (1 Kings 10:1-13; 2 Chron. 9:1-9). The Kebre Negest (The Glory of the Kings), which was composed around A.D. 1320 with both pre-Christian and Christian materials, recounts the visit of the queen of Sheba to King Solomon in Jerusalem. It is believed that her relationship with King Solomon resulted in the birth of a son. According to tradition, this son, who was named Manilek, visited his father Solomon when he grew up, and King Solomon sent him back to Ethiopia accompanied by some Israelites to serve him, with Levites as priests who brought back the ark of the covenant. From then onward, Judaism was practiced in Ethiopia.[6]

In the New Testament, Acts 8:26-40 tells us that a certain eunuch, the treasurer of Queen Candace of Ethiopia, went to Jerusalem to worship the God of Israel. There he met Philip, who baptized him. According to tradition, he returned home and evangelized his people. St. Frumentius played a key role in the conversion of Emperor Ezana around A.D. 330. A Greek inscription belonging to Ezana states: "In the faith of God and the power of the Father, the Son and the Holy Ghost." From henceforth and even to the present, Christianity has played a prominent role in the national life of Ethiopians. Unlike other lands, Christianity came through the royal families and then to the ordinary people. The kings and especially the late emperor Haile Selassie were not only seen as the political head but also the spiritual leader. It is for this reason that Haile Selassie was buried in the Ethiopian Orthodox Church in Addis Ababa. For our particular interest, Ethiopian Christianity emerged in the context of the Arian controversy when the divinity of Christ was hotly debated. The Ethiopian church stood by the side of Athanasius and the Nicene Creed, which affirmed the full deity of Christ and also affirmed the threeness of the Godhead, Father, Son, and Holy Spirit. The Ethiopian Orthodox Church proudly stands in the tradition of the Nicene Creed and publicly displays its belief in the Trinity — in fact the most prominent church in Addis Ababa, where

---

6. D. A. Hubbard, "Queen Sheba," in the *International Standard Bible Encyclopedia*, ed. Geoffrey W. Bromiley (Grand Rapids: Eerdmans, 1988), 4:8-10; D. Harvey, "Sheba, Queen of," in *Interpreter's Dictionary of the Bible*, ed. George A. Buttrick (Nashville: Abingdon, 1962), 4:311-12.

the late emperor Haile Selassie is buried, is called "The Trinity Ortho-dox Ethiopian Church."[7]

The theology of the Trinity, as we have seen, is a very pronounced aspect of the Ethiopian church. The Trinity is not only stated in their books but also expressed in church paintings. These images and paint-ings are meant to be kept before the eyes of the worshiper's prayerful gaze, to inspire prayer, meditation, and devotion. They are intended for the worshiper for two ways of seeing, "to see and to be seen." It is believed that when praying in front of the paintings, not only are wor-shipers looking at pictures, but the spirit of the subject of the pictures is also looking at worshipers at the same time.

III. Islamic Concept of God

The African Christian cannot discuss the Trinity without interacting with Islam, whose understanding of God sharply contrasts with the Christian view of God. Often, these two major religions collide head-on over their contrasting views of God. Islam was founded in the seventh century and borrowed some of its beliefs from Judaism and Christian-ity. From Judaism, it stresses absolute monotheism to the exclusion of any plurality within the Godhead. Many heresies such as Arianism and other heretical views were already prevalent in the seventh and eighth centuries. The major thrust of Islam is its teaching on God, and this has become the major sour point with Christianity. Robert Letham writes, "Its doctrine of God is the major weakness of Islam. It is the root of all other problems. It is here that the Christian apologete and evangelist can probe, with sensitivity and wisdom. While the Trinity is one of the major stumbling blocks to Muslims turning to Christ, it must be present-ed with intelligence and skill."[8] In Islam, therefore, the idea of a Trinity is repugnant and unacceptable (see the Qur'an 4:471; 5:76). Allah is one, Islam teaches, and cannot have a son, for it is not befitting for God to

---

7. Selassie, *Church of Ethiopia*; Lule Melaku, *History of the Ethiopian Orthodox Tewahedo Church: From the Reign of Emperor Caleb to the End of the Zagwe Dynasty and from the Classical (Golden) Age to the Present* (Addis Ababa: Elleni, 2010), parts two and three; Bantalem Tadesse, *A Guide to the Intangible Treasures of Ethiopian Orthodox Tewahido Church: Historic Perspectives and Symbolic Interpretations of Festivals* (Addis Ababa: Kalu, 2010).

8. Robert Letham, *The Holy Trinity in Scripture, History, Theology and Worship* (Phillips-burg, N.J.: P&R, 2004), p. 446.

have a son. Despite Islam's rejection of the Trinity, it is a critical element of Christian faith and nonnegotiable in reaching out to Muslims. Without going into too much discussion, what is most productive in dialogue with Muslims is to discuss the divine attributes of Christ, which are also found in God. These include, among others, creation (see Qur'an 4:171; 3:49; 5:11; 19:34; 22;34; 22:73; cf. John 1:1-5), sovereignty (Qr. 3:45-50; cf. Mark 4:37-41), holiness (Qur'an 3:45; 19:16-19; cf. Luke 7:48; John 1:29), omniscience (Qur'an 4:171; cf. Mic. 5:2; John 8:58); Judge (Qur'an 4:158; 43:61; 4:78-80; cf. Matt. 24–25; Rev. 21–22).

One attribute of God that is lacking in Islam is the concept of God as love. Islam emphasizes the justice and power of God and that God or "Allah cannot love."[9] Love cannot be found in a monad god, but can only be properly expressed among persons. This is readily available within the Godhead and has also been exhibited toward his created world: "God so loved the world that he gave his only begotten son" (John 3:16).

IV. Distortions of the Trinity in Contemporary African Christianity

The heresies of the Trinity were not only found in the early church and the West; they are duplicated today, and some new variations have arisen. We need only mention a few. Theism holds to belief in God and nothing more. African Christians are susceptible to this error due to their cultural worldview, which does not have a clear understanding of the triune God. The triune God easily loses its uniqueness in a general and ambiguous belief in God. In many instances, believers feel comfortable just referring to God as the supernatural or the supreme God. This vague theism is found in interreligious discussions with other faiths such as African Traditional Religions, Jehovah's Witnesses, and Islam. This is done in order to remove offense to those who are nontrinitarian. While it is true that Christians need not be unnecessarily provocative, the Christian cannot afford to downplay the triune confession of God; otherwise he will have reduced Christianity to just another theistic religion.

Modalism is the belief that God is one but has manifested himself in three modes at various historical moments, for example, that God

9. Letham, *Holy Trinity*, p. 444.

revealed himself as the Father in the Old Testament period, as Jesus in the New Testament, and as the Holy Spirit in the church age. This modalistic view of God has been quite common, especially among the older version of African Initiated Churches that did not have the benefit of formal training in theology. In its early stages, the Cherubim and Seraphim Church held to this version of modalism. Apostle Abana allocates the three ages to the three persons, stating, "As the names are three, so also is the Bible divided into three parts: the name of the Father means God the Father and refers to Genesis through Malachi; the name of the Son means Jesus Christ and refers to Matthew through Jude; and the name of the Holy Ghost refers to Revelation, which is the last book of the Bible."[10] Captain Christianah Abiodun Emanuel, one of the pioneers of the Cherubim and Seraphim movements, holds the same view. This is the heresy of modalism, which the early church condemned.

Unitarianism of the Spirit is a reductionistic posture that emphasizes the third person of the Trinity, the Holy Spirit. Modern African Christianity, particularly Pentecostal and charismatic movements, revolve around the experience of the Holy Spirit. The prayers by ministers and evangelists of certain Christian groups and individuals are a clear indication that there is a move toward a unitarianism of the Spirit. While the church certainly needs to experience the Holy Spirit's gifts, it is equally dangerous to overemphasize this aspect to the detriment of God the Father and God the Son. The Spirit who empowers reconciliation and liberation is the Spirit of Christ and of the one Christ called "Abba, Father."

Jesusology is another distortion of the use and name of Jesus in Christian worship. Just as in the case of the Holy Spirit, there has been a development in recent years in the use of the name of Jesus as a magical means of getting answers to prayer. Apart from the baptismal formula, dedications, consecrations, and benedictions – which generally remain trinitarian – the church and believers use the name of Jesus in total disregard of the triune God in worship and prayer.

In a functional Trinity view, the triune God is used in some instances as a means of achieving personal needs. In prayers and worship, one often has the feeling that the names of God, especially the Son and the Holy Spirit, are used as a magical means to acquire personal needs

10. J. Akinyele Omoyajowo, *Cherubim and Seraphim: The History of an African Independent Church* (New York: Nok, 1982), p. 101.

such as guidance, protection, and judgment against perceived or even real enemies. The phrase "in the name of Jesus" is invoked by the believer in prayer over and over to emphasize the power in Jesus' name. The blood of Jesus is used to protect children from spiritual attack, for protection against accidents, and so on. The Holy Spirit is invoked to punish enemies or opposition. The selection of verses of Scripture to justify such use is rampant in churches. Selective and wrong use of the triune God in prayers and worship is a distortion.

V. The Knowledge of God

For the Christian faith, divine revelation is a fundamental belief without which Christianity has no basis for existence. Without the self-disclosure of God to his creation, creation would not be able to know anything about God. Revelation in the strictest sense means God's initiative, disclosure, and unveiling. Divine revelation is therefore cardinal to the Christian religion. Its understanding of revelation is set forth in the Bible, the Word of God. Our understanding of revelation as Christians ultimately must be drawn from an understanding of Scripture, the primary vehicle of divine revelation. However, since revelation has also been experienced by human beings in every culture, it is critical that we understand revelation from an African perspective and how this Christian experience relates to divine revelation. The only true source of knowledge about God is his personal revelation of himself in Jesus Christ and the recording of that revelation in the inspired, inerrant, and infallible Holy Scriptures. Indeed, Scripture insists that knowledge of a personal and sovereign God combined with worship of him through other divinities boils down to idolatry: "For although they knew God, they neither glorified him as God nor gave thanks to him, but their thinking became futile and their foolish hearts were darkened. . . . They exchanged the truth about God for a lie, and worshiped and served created things rather than the Creator" (Rom. 1:21-25).

VI. The God of the Scriptures and Trinity in History

The Bible teaches that God is self-existent. When Moses asks God who he is, God simply replies, "I AM WHO I AM" (Exod. 3:13-14). The psalmist

63

regards any questioning of the fact of God's existence as foolishness (Ps. 14:1), and most Africans would agree. There is thus no need to explore the proofs of the existence of God in this work. What is important is to seek to understand more about God, and the only way to achieve such understanding is to examine his self-revelation in his written Word. When we do this, we discover that God exists in Trinity, is transcendent and immanent, sovereign, omnipotent, holy, just, and loving.

If there is one thing that our brief history brings to mind immediately, especially from the Ethiopian Orthodox Church, it is that the contemporary church in Africa does not lose touch or interest in the history or tradition of her past. There are several advantages in looking back at the history and the traditions of the church.

First of all, it reminds the church of her roots and traditions and helps us to tread in its paths. It is unfortunate that the history of missions often stops with the pioneers who brought the gospel to Africans from the United States, Canada, England, Australia, and so on but never traces its faith to, or builds it on, its traditions. The consequence, of course, is that the contemporary African church neither cares nor knows the beliefs, traditions, and roots of its forebears. Very few church members know anything beyond the early Christian missionaries and converts, and clearly almost nothing about the history of the early church.

Second, as a consequence of the above point, contemporary African churches do not know the difference between right and wrong belief, orthodox and heretical teachings. The Ethiopian Orthodox Church, which emphasizes right belief going back to the early history of the church, always ensures through its recitation of them that these beliefs are neither abandoned nor discontinued in church life and practice.

Third, reminding ourselves of the past ensures continuity with the past traditions that the church must adhere to. The church in Africa lacks continuity with the past traditions. Every church comes and goes with its own inventions of what it considers right or wrong belief. We must remind ourselves that the church of Jesus Christ did not begin today, and we must appreciate and carry on the traditions of the past and pass it on to future generations.

All these historic creeds affirm trinitarian theology, which should be the universal teaching of the Christian church. The church in Africa must also be seen as affirming, teaching, and upholding these creeds.

The Triune God in Spirituality

The very essence of Christianity is trinitarian. Every aspect of the Christian life and experience is and must be rooted in the Father, the Son, and the Holy Spirit. One would have a very truncated view of the Christian life without the Trinity. Our salvation cannot be understood without it. The Father loved us, Jesus died for us, and the Holy Spirit lives and enables us to understand the Word and live life in accordance with the will of God. "A living relationship with God requires that each of the persons be honored and adored in the context of their revealed relations with each other. The nature of our response in worship is to be shaped by the reality of the one we worship."[11] The clear teaching of Scripture is that we pray to the Father, in the name of Jesus Christ, and by the enablement of the Holy Spirit. However, one finds that in these days, this order is not observed, as believers often confuse it or ignore it in prayer. For example, it is quite common to hear worshipers pray to the Holy Spirit to take vengeance on their enemies. In the New Testament, the Father is addressed through the Son, by the power of the Holy Spirit.

VII. The Triune God in Worship

True worship is the acknowledgment and adoration of the Father, Son, and Holy Spirit – very trinitarian (Eph. 2:18). "Prayer, worship, and communion with God are by definition Trinitarian. As the Father has made himself known through the Son 'for us and our salvation' in or by the Spirit, so we are all caught up in this reverse movement. We live, move, and have our being in a pervasively Trinitarian atmosphere."[12] One essential aspect of worship is prayers to the triune God (John 4:24; Rev. 5:11).[13] Another is hymns. Our songs in worship should reflect our trinitarian understanding of God. Charles Wesley (1707-88) composed a hymn in 1746 that does just this, something Christians would do well to emulate in their song-making and worship.

---

11. Letham, *Holy Trinity,* p. 419.
12. Letham, *Holy Trinity,* pp. 7-8.
13. Letham, *Holy Trinity,* pp. 412, 419.

Father of Mankind, Be ever ador'd:
Thy Mercy we find, In sending our Lord,
To ransom and bless us; Thy Goodness we praise,
For sending in Jesus, Salvation by Grace.

O Son of His Love, Who deignest to die,
Our Curse to remove, Our Pardon to buy;
Accept our Thanksgiving, Almighty to save,
Who openest Heaven, To all that believe.

O Spirit of Love, Of Health, and Power,
Thy working we prove; Thy Grace we adore,
Whose inward Revealing applies our Lord's Blood,
Attesting and sealing us Children of God.

This hymn clearly articulates the drama of salvation. Without a clear understanding of the Father, Son, and Holy Spirit, our understanding of salvation will be incomplete. Songs should play a key role in clarifying our redemption. Choruses and short songs that are commonplace in African churches should reflect this trinitarian belief among believers.

Conclusion

First, the African church must recover its past, its history, and its traditions. The church in Africa does not stand in isolation from the church Christ has been building over the centuries. Though the primary and fundamental source of the Christian life is Holy Scripture, we must not forget that from the Old Testament to the New Testament to the early church and succeeding generations, Christ has been at work in his church. The church has grappled with many issues and drawn some universal conclusions. These universal conclusions, which include among others the Trinity and the hypostatic union, are important beliefs and considered orthodox (right doctrine) not only for past generations of believers but even for today. The Ethiopian Orthodox Church is a model of such a church that has held on to this orthodox belief and practice.

Second, the church in Africa must consciously and deliberately evolve ways of reintroducing and retrenching the belief in and practice of the Trinity as an essential part of the church. Some of these methods may include recitation of the Apostles' and the Nicene Creeds every Sunday. The Ethiopian Orthodox Church makes pictures of the Trinity, and this helps believers and worshipers to keep trinitarian theology in view. In spite of its shortcomings, it is true that a picture is worth more than a thousand words. In a nonliterate society, the idea of pictures sends the message across very distinctly. This is more so when biblical exposition and recitation of church creeds go hand in hand, and this ought to provide safeguards against misconstruing such images. Of course rote memory can be counterproductive, but when included in songs, praise, or storytelling about the early church, one can have a balanced position.

Third, the pulpit should take the lead on the exposition of the theology of the Trinity. Many believers are not able to remember when their pastor preached on the Trinity except when saying the benediction, wedding blessings, or launching or dedicating a church building, musical instrument, or a home. The pulpit must take center stage in helping the congregation to know what the church has believed over the years and what the Bible clearly teaches. Letham does not underemphasize the importance of preaching. "Chief of all, the Trinity must be preached and must shape preaching. Preaching is the highest point of worship. Not only must the Trinity be preached, but all preaching must be shaped by the active recognition that the God whose word is so proclaimed is triune. A Trinitarian mindset must become as integral to the preacher as the air we breathe. The most practical preaching is that which enables us to advance in our knowledge of the God who is three persons."[14]

Fourth, materials and manuals about the Trinity should be made available to all the believers. Those who become full members should be conversant with the essentials of the church, which must include teaching on the Trinity. Believers need to be conversant with the Apostles' Creed, the Nicene Creed, and the Athanasian Creed.

Fifth, and finally, Christians in Africa must reinstate and develop a trinitarian theology that is relevant to the rise of an aggressive and violent Islam. Militant Islam falls short of a loving and caring God as provided in a trinitarian theology that depicts God as loving and caring, who loves to save and not to kill his enemies.

Ultimately, grasping God's triunity is about God, not about believers or even ourselves. The doxology says it very well.

14. Letham, *Holy Trinity*, p. 423.

Praise God from whom all blessings flow,
Praise Him all his creatures here below,
Praise him above you heavenly hosts,
Praise Father, Son and Holy Ghost,
Amen.

Further Reading

Gerald Bray, *Creeds, Councils and Christ: The Continuity Between Scripture and Orthodoxy in the First Five Centuries* (Leicester, U.K.: Inter-Varsity Press, 1984).

Jean Marc Ela, *My Faith as an African*, trans. John P. Brown and Susan Perry (Maryknoll, N.Y.: Orbis, 1981).

Bolaji Idowu, *Towards an Indigenous Church* (London: Oxford University Press, 1965).

James Owino Kombo, *The Doctrine of God in African Christian Thought: The Holy Trinity, Theological Hermeneutics and the African Intellectual Culture* (The Netherlands: Hotei, 2007).

———, "The Trinity in Africa," *Journal of Reformed Theology* 3 (2009): 125-43.

Samuel Waje Kunhiyop, *African Christian Ethics* (Grand Rapids: Zondervan, 2008).

———, *African Christian Theology* (Grand Rapids: Zondervan, 2012).

Robert Letham, *The Holy Trinity in Scripture, History, Theology, and Worship* (Phillipsburg, N.J.: P&R, 2004).

J. S. Mangayi and J. Buitendag, "A Critical Analysis of African Traditional Religion and the Trinity," *Teologiese Studies/Theological Studies* 69 (2013): http://www.hts.org.za/index.php/HTS/article/view/1934/3679.

A. Okechukwu Ogbonnaya, *On Communitarian Divinity: An African Interpretation of the Trinity* (St. Paul: Paragon, 1998).

J. Akinyele Omojajowo, *Cherubim and Seraphim: The History of an African Independent Church* (New York: Nok, 1982).

Edward Geoffrey Parrinder, *African Traditional Religion* (Westport, Conn.: Greenwood, 1970).

Sergew Hable Sellassie, *The Church of Ethiopia: A Panorama of History and Spiritual Life* (Addis Ababa: Ethiopian Orthodox Church, 1997).

John Thurmer, *A Detection of the Trinity* (Exeter: Paternoster, 1984).

CHAPTER 4

The Trinity as Gospel

Antonio González

ABSTRACT

The divinity of Jesus is not a contradiction to Jewish monotheism, but rather a way of its messianic fulfillment. Jewish monotheism was not a simple metaphysical affirmation of the uniqueness of God, but originated as an affirmation of the exclusive rule of God. Therefore, all other sources of power were radically called into question in the context of Jewish monotheism, including the power of the king. This is the root of the historical and theological difficulties that the Hebrew Bible shows when it comes to understand and justify the existence of Israel as a state. Jesus' message about the kingdom of God should be understood against the background of this affirmation of the exclusive rule of God. And this is also the reason why the resurrected and exalted Jesus could not be understood as an intermediate being between humanity and God. In this context, it is comprehensible why the inclusion of Jesus in the divinity of the only God took place so early, and in a Jewish context.

The doctrine of the Trinity belongs to the core of Christian beliefs. Nevertheless, for some Christians and many non-Christians, the Trinity is a strange entity in the history of monotheism. Many would suspect that the doctrine of the Trinity is the result of the introduction of Christianity in the Hellenistic world of the first centuries of our era. In this context, the first Gentile Christians, principally Paul, would have been the main culprits in the beginning of the exaltation of Jesus as a heavenly figure, thereby opening in this way the possibility of the subsequent proclamation of Jesus as "God." This proclamation, supposedly done for the first time by the early church councils,[1] also included the idea of the deity of the Holy Spirit and therefore became the ground for the doctrine of the Trinity.

I. Latin American Context

We can observe various responses to these difficulties within the Latin American context. All of them seek to underscore the relevance of the Trinity for the present moment in Latin America, especially for the millions who live under oppressive situations. In this sense we could say that all the different ways we think about the Trinity respond to what we may call the "perspective of the poor." This is a characteristic of liberation theology, although it is found in various other theological forms.

In the first place, in some quarters the doctrine of the Trinity has been accepted as a late development that now has practically become insignificant for the church. Clearly there is an appreciation of the fact that in the past speculative theology used trinitarian categories. These became a way to think about the implications of the fact that God had manifested himself in Jesus Christ. However, in the present time the important consideration is not the speculation about the character of God himself but rather to center our attention on Jesus Christ. This means that we cannot start from a previous concept of God, including the doctrine of the Trinity, but we must begin with Jesus Christ. The proclamation of Jesus' divinity would not, in this sense, mean that Jesus is God but rather affirms that God is Jesus, that is to say, only in Jesus can we know who God is. This sense, in spite of being important, leaves opaque the very idea of the Trinity, and some have consequently considered it to be radically obsolete. Rather, what is important is to underline the humanity of Jesus and his importance as a model for discipleship.

In liberation theology we also encounter a second perspective regarding the Trinity, which, instead of considering it obsolete, values it as essential to Christian thought. From this perspective, pure mono-

1. Especially the Councils of Nicaea (325) and Constantinople (381).

theism holds within it a tendency toward legitimizing oppression. The image of one unique God in the heavens tends to favor totalitarian or dictatorial government in the land: only one can govern. In this point we can clearly see the influence of Erik Peterson's thesis,[2] which wrestled with monotheism's import in the context of national socialism. In the case of liberation theology, some extended this analysis to the structures of their own church. The image of an exclusive government in heaven favored authoritarian models in the church, with exclusive power centered on one person, the same as what occurs when the church concedes all the government's power to one person. In the face of these celestial images that legitimate political or ecclesiastical power, this stream of liberation theology emphasizes the image of the Trinity as community. And if God is a community, this favors the establishment of egalitarian relations on earth that reflect the reality of God. On the other hand, every authoritarian structure on earth comes under critique in the light of the communitarian and egalitarian God of the Trinity.[3]

In my view, these two lines of thinking need to be revised for various reasons. In the first place, both lines of reflection presuppose that divine revelation is structured like a mirror, such that what we see on earth is in some way a reflection of the model, which is in heaven. Therefore some assert that what we know about God is only that which is reflected in Christ, or they affirm the idea that a celestial model is paradigmatic for earthly governmental structures. Second, we have to ask if this idea of a celestial "model" or "paradigm" does greater justice to the "perspective of the poor," as emphasized repeatedly in Latin American theology. How does a celestial model help those who are oppressed in their earthly life? And, in the third place, we should question the idea, commonly held in Latin American theology, that the Trinity comes from a later speculation in the history of theology, given that its biblical foundations are weak.

At this point something needs to be said about those biblical foundations. As we know, the Pauline Letters represent the most complete ancient collection of New Testament writings. However, perceptions

---

2. See Erik Peterson, *Der Monotheismus als politisches Problem: ein Beitrag zur Geschichte der politischen Theologie im Imperium Romanum* (Leipzig: Hegner, 1935).

3. See Leonardo Boff, "Trinidad," in *Mysterium liberationis: Conceptos fundamentales de la teología de la liberación*, ed. Jon Sobrino and Ignacio Ellacuría (Madrid: Trotta, 1990), pp. 513-30, esp. pp. 514-16.

about Paul are changing significantly in two fundamental ways. On one hand, current Pauline scholarship stresses the so-called new perspective on Paul.[4] According to this perspective, in its many variants, Paul belonged completely to the Jewish world, and was by no means trying to build some kind of synthesis between the Hebraic faith and the Hellenistic world with its plurality of gods. On the other hand, many New Testament scholars are now ready to admit that the proclamation of Jesus' deity was by no means a slow process, which would have only taken place when Christianity was adapted to Hellenistic culture. Many scholars think that the first Christians, even those before Paul, did in fact believe Jesus belonged to the deity of God.[5]

How is this possible? How could a group of Jewish believers come so early to proclaim the deity of the Messiah? These results are even stranger when we recognize that these early Christians were by no means thinking that they were giving up the story of strict Old Testament monotheism.[6]

Some have tried to solve these difficulties by affirming that the Jewish monotheism of the first century was not as strict as it became later, this development being partly due to the discussions in rabbinic Judaism against the Christian movement. In this sense, some have thought that some figures like the divine Wisdom could be understood as precedents and conditions that made the "high" Christology of the New Testament possible.[7] The problem is that such figures as Wisdom, although present, are relatively scarce in the New Testament writings. For a growing number of scholars, these intermediate figures played no role in the rapid development of New Testament Christology and are not especially relevant for the doctrine of the Trinity.[8]

4. Beginning with E. P. Sanders's book *Paul and Palestinian Judaism: A Comparison of Patterns of Religion* (Philadelphia: Fortress, 1977). The term "new perspective" was later coined by James D. G. Dunn.

5. See N. T. Wright, *Paul in Fresh Perspective* (Minneapolis: Fortress, 2005). See also Larry Hurtado, *Lord Jesus Christ: Devotion to Jesus in Earliest Christianity* (Grand Rapids: Eerdmans, 2003).

6. See Gordon D. Fee, *Pauline Christology: An Exegetical-Theological Study* (Peabody, Mass.: Hendrickson, 2007).

7. See Martin Hengel, *Der Sohn Gottes: Die Entstehung der Christologie und die jüdisch-hellenistische Religionsgeschichte*, 2nd ed. (Tübingen: Mohr Siebeck, 1977).

8. See Richard Bauckham, *Jesus and the God of Israel: God Crucified and Other Studies on the New Testament's Christology of Divine Identity* (Grand Rapids: Eerdmans, 2008). See also the already quoted book of Fee, *Pauline Christology*, pp. 595-630.

Following and radicalizing the path opened by authors like Richard Bauckham, Gordon Fee, and N. T. Wright, I will try to show that the reasons for the early development of Christology in a mainly Jewish monotheistic milieu are directly related, not with the possible Jewish ideas of intermediate beings, but with the central New Testament ideas about the kingdom of God and the messianic position of Jesus. As a result of this, early Christian belief in the deity of Jesus would need to be thought in complete continuity with Old Testament monotheism. If such is the case, the doctrine of the Trinity would not be a strange addition to the history of monotheism but rather the culmination of this history. Let us think about this in more detail.

II. Monotheistic Exclusivity

To properly understand the development of the Christian doctrine of God, it is essential to understand the meaning of God's exclusivity in the Hebrew Scriptures. The monotheism of Israel is not a result of philosophical speculation about the unity of God. On the contrary, it is God's saving action in the history of Israel that brings about the idea of the uniqueness of God. And here the idea of God's kingdom, God's rule over Israel, plays a decisive role.

To see this, we can look at the actual canon of the Torah and examine the place where the idea of God's kingdom appears for the first time. It is in the book of Exodus just at the moment when the people of God arrive safely at the other side of the sea. Moses then sings, and at the end of his song he proclaims: "The Lord will reign forever and ever" (Exod. 15:18). The place of this affirmation is extremely significant. It is when the rule of Pharaoh is broken, when his sovereignty does not reach God's people, that the people can truly proclaim that God is now their king, and that he will be forever. The rule of God, the kingdom of God, reveals itself as an exclusive rule, which is incompatible with the rule of Pharaoh.

It is important to observe that we have a structure here that is opposite to the structure of myths. According to Mircea Eliade, the myths of religions usually regard the images of the gods in heaven as some kind of model or paradigm of the realities on earth.[9] For example, the

---

9. See Mircea Eliade, *Aspects du Mythe* (Paris: Gallimard, 1963).

pantheon of the gods in heaven is the paradigm of the royal court of the "real" kings of Mesopotamia.[10] A female goddess in heaven is the model of a priestess, or a queen, and so on. This is of course also a structure of ideological justification. The king god explains and blesses the rule and power of his human image on earth.

What we see in the Hebrew Scriptures is a wholly different structure. The God of Israel is able to have a direct relationship with his people, without intermediate figures. If God is king, the people of God do not need another king. God can rule his people directly, as long as his people desire to be ruled by God. This is the reason why, in the first book of Samuel, the introduction of state and monarchy is a big problem. As God says to the prophet, the people who ask for a king are not just rejecting Samuel, they are rejecting God himself as their king (1 Sam. 8:7).[11]

We can see this same structure in other areas. The idea of God being a warrior, a "Lord of the hosts," is the basis for the affirmation that the people do not need to prepare for war. God will fight the battles of his people (Exod. 14:14). That is why the people should reduce their army and trust God, who will take care of their defense. Again, the God in heaven does not work as a heavenly paradigm, designed to justify the warriors on earth. On the contrary: because God is a warrior, the people would not need to worry about war.[12] The same can be said about the image of God as master. God became a master of all the Israelites when he redeemed them from slavery in Egypt, and this is the very reason to limit slavery in Israel (Lev. 25:54-55).

In short, the direct rule of God means that God assumes the roles of domination. By doing this, these roles are limited or excluded from his people. The people of God are designed in the Torah like brothers and sisters, and among them there should not be significant social differences. This is the reason for the many social measures that we can find in the Torah.[13] We can also say that the connection between monotheism and social justice is a direct one. Social justice is not a sec-

---

10. Jean Bottéro, *La plus vieille religion: En Mésopotamie* (Paris: Gallimard, 1998).

11. See Norbert Lohfink, *Das Jüdische am Christentum: Die verlorene Dimension* (Freiburg im Breisgau: Herder, 1987), pp. 71-102.

12. John Howard Yoder, *The Original Revolution: Essays on Christian Pacifism* (Scottdale, Pa.: Herald Press, 2003).

13. Exod. 21:1-11; 23:12; Lev. 25:8-55; Deut. 15:1-18; 23:15. In Deut. 26:12-15 we have "the first known tax for a social program," according to Frank Crüsemann, *The Torah: Theology and Social History of Old Testament Law* (Edinburgh: T&T Clark, 1996), p. 218.

ondary consequence of monotheism, but the very expression of God's direct and exclusive rule over his people. This is precisely what the true prophets of Israel said.

Here we can see a decisive difference with Greek philosophical theism. For the Greek philosophers, the affirmation of some sort of Supreme Being was always compatible with the idea that many other realities could be considered divine, somehow participating in the same divine character. Instead, biblical monotheism is exclusive, and this exclusivity is directly related to the idea of an exclusive rule of God.

In due time, this exclusive rule of God came to embrace all peoples and all realities. God was perceived as the king, not only over Israel, but also as the king who rules the entire history of humankind. At the same time, this universal rule is the rule of a Creator God, who does not need any other kind of eternal realities beside him. He creates all things, and all things are created realities. No reality, no star, no moon, no sun, no person, no animal, can therefore aspire to be some kind of companion or alternative to God (Gen. 1:14-19).

Here we encounter something different from what has been thought in European theology, from Peterson to Moltmann, and also something different from what Latin American theology assumed when it wanted to situate itself with the "perspective of the poor." In the history of Israel, the idea of one exclusive God, instead of signifying the legitimation of authoritarian forms of power on earth, was the means by which those powers were critiqued. A good part of Latin American theology seems to have continued thinking in this way of a celestial image that functions as a "paradigm" for its earthly reflection, a thought common in the history of religions. But for Israel, if God is the king over his people, there is no place for the other kings. For this precise reason it is not strange that Jesus assumes the category of the "kingdom of God" as the central theme of his proclamation.

III. Jesus and the Exclusivity of God

These Hebrew ideas about God are essential if we are to understand the early and quick development of Christian Christology and the basis of the doctrine of the Trinity. Although usually forgotten, the Old Testament is essential for the doctrine of the Trinity. Without the Hebrew Scriptures, it is impossible to understand the Christian doctrine of God.

When we read the Hebrew Scriptures as a whole, we cannot avoid a sense of failure. The people of God were not able to exist among the nations as a living testimony of the exclusivity of God. The "Deuteronomistic" writers and the prophets blame the people as a whole, and specifically the kings, for this disaster. The people, again and again, forsake the exclusivity of God and the fulfilling of the Torah. For many Jews of the first centuries, there had been no real restoration after exile.[14]

In this context, Jesus preaches the gospel of the kingdom of God (Mark 1:15). The gospel is the good news of God coming to rule over his people.[15] This rule is again a direct one. The kingdom of God is close. Saying this, Jesus is connecting with the hopes expressed by the prophets concerning a direct rule of God over his people (Jer. 23:1-8; Ezek. 34:1-22).[16] To put it briefly, we can see this direct rule of God in four aspects of Jesus' teaching and activity.

a) Jesus teaches about God as Father, an image already present, but not very developed in the Hebrew Bible. God's rule is like the benevolent rule of a paterfamilias, who takes care of his people. As a matter of fact, Jesus' followers probably organized themselves in houses. In those houses it was possible to share goods, help each other, forgive debts, and so on. But these houses had no other father than God. Again, the rule of God is exclusive. Against what feminist theology used to think, if God is Father, patriarchalism has no place. And against what was thought in the first currents of liberation theology, the image of God as Father, far from favoring the patriarchalism of traditional agrarian societies[17] or ecclesial patriarchalism, instead justly critiques them. Jesus' disciples should not call anybody "father," because they have only one Father in heaven (Matt. 23:9). A person entering the kingdom of God may leave father, mother, brothers, and sisters, but he or she will recover all of them, hundreds of times, except the fathers (Mark 10:29-30).

b) Jesus depicts God as a landowner. As a matter of fact, this is the

---

14. See N. T. Wright, *The New Testament and the People of God* (Minneapolis: Fortress, 1992), pp. 268-71.

15. See N. T. Wright, "Paul and Caesar: A New Reading of Romans," in *A Royal Priesthood: The Use of the Bible Ethically and Politically*, ed. Craig Bartholomew (Carlisle: Paternoster, 2002), pp. 173-93.

16. Note that Ezekiel, after affirming the future direct sovereignty of God over his people, does not call the future David "king," but only "prince," in Ezek. 34:24.

17. As Boff suggested in "Trinidad," p. 515.

subject of many of his parables.[18] In them, Jesus connects with the Old Testament image of God as the real owner of the land and the farmers just being tenants of their fields (Lev. 25:23-24). This meant that all the people will come back to the lands of their ancestors after a period of forty-nine years, putting an end to extreme social differences (Lev. 25:8-22). In Jesus' parables, the coming of the kingdom is compared to the coming of the real owner of the land. And this is again an exclusive process. God, as the real owner, will take back his own land, which is now in the hands of tenants who have usurped a land that does not belong to them. In other words: if God is landowner, the time for other landowners is limited.

If we situate ourselves in the "perspective of the poor," as liberation theology suggests, now we truly have good news for the poor. The good news for the poor does not consist in proposing a celestial model that should be imitated. The good news is such when we hear the announcement of what God has done in our favor. The proclamation that God is the King who has returned to reign, and that he is the landowner who returns to claim his land, announces precisely the beginning of the end of oppression.

c) In this context we can also understand Jesus' nonviolence. If God is king, he will protect his people. The people only have to trust God. If you take this Old Testament teaching to its ultimate fulfillment, you will not reduce the army, as Gideon did (Judg. 7:1-25), or as Deuteronomy teaches (Deut. 17:14-20). Radical faith in God's protection means that Jesus' followers will not have any army. They will trust God, looking for new and creative ways to act in front of their enemies (Matt. 5:38-48). The exclusive kingdom of the mighty God makes warriors unnecessary.

Here we also encounter the necessity of radicalizing some of the common ideas found in Latin American theology. Like the majority of Christian theologians from the sixth century onward, liberation theology understood that, in certain circumstances, it was legitimate to resort to violence against the oppressor. With that, liberation theology did nothing more than apply the traditional doctrine of the "just war" to revolutionary situations, something Augustine of Hippo, who took it from Cicero, utilized to legitimate the new "Christian" emperors' recourse to violence. The similar revolutionary experience in Latin

---

18. Matt. 20:1-16; Mark 12:1-10; 13:33-37; Luke 12:35-38, 42-46; 15:11-32; 16:1-9; 17:7-10.

America belies the wisdom of this option. In reality, the radical discipleship of Jesus, which liberation theology insistently proposes, and the very idea of the kingdom of God must rather be carried out in postures that are consequently pacifist.

d) This context of the direct and exclusive kingdom of God makes us understand what has usually been called the "messianic secret." The reason for this secret is not the assumption that Jesus did not understand himself as Messiah, and only the disciples did after the resurrection. Rather, the reason for this secret is that Jesus did not like the "political" or the "violent" ideas about a Messiah. The problem is more deeply theological. Jesus was proclaiming the coming of the kingdom, and this was an exclusive kingdom. But the main meaning of Messiah for first-century Jews was none other than the anointed king, wherein lies the problem. If this kingdom of God is a direct and exclusive one, there is little room for another king in it.

As a matter of fact, many symbolic actions of Jesus, such as his own baptism and the election and sending of the Twelve, are clear allusions to the "young" Israel, the Israel that existed without state or king for almost two hundred years.

Here we have great insight into the messianic consciousness of Jesus. At the decisive moments, Jesus did not deny that he was the expected Messiah. But, at the same time, he corrected this title with the image of the Son of Man (Mark 8:27-33; 14:61-62). The Son of Man, as is well known, is not only an image of humility. On the contrary, the strange figure of the Son of Man from chapter 7 of the book of Daniel prompts interesting associations:

a) The Son of Man is a human image, in contrast to the history of empires in the human story, which represent themselves as beasts (lions, leopards, tigers, eagles, dragons, etc.), because they are beasts. The kingdom of God is a human kingdom, a kingdom with a human face.

b) The Son of Man shares his kingdom. The dominion is given to the Son of Man, but also to the people of the saints of the Most High (Dan. 7:18). This shared kingdom is an important motif in Jesus' preaching and also for early Christians.[19]

---

19. Matt. 17:25-27; 18:28; 2 Tim. 2:12; Rev. 5:10; see Gerd Theissen and Annette Merz, *Der historische Jesus: Ein Lehrbuch* (Göttingen: Vandenhoeck & Ruprecht, 1996).

c) The Son of Man is depicted as moving toward the throne of God. Here we also approach the question of the deity of Jesus.

IV. Resurrection as Messianic Exaltation

The resurrection of Jesus was interpreted very early as messianic exaltation. By his resurrection, Jesus was declared Messiah (Rom. 1:4), solving this issue once and for all. This declaration as Messiah obviously means that Jesus is now in a ruling position. Jesus has been declared king. Not a king in the palaces of Jerusalem, but a king who now rules from heaven. As Paul puts it, Jesus is "at the right hand of God" (Rom. 8:34). It seems from this text that Paul is presupposing that the Christians of Rome, whom he has not yet met, already share this knowledge.

Along this line, many other texts suppose that Jesus, now resurrected, shares the very ruling position of God. Some texts speak about only one throne in heaven, shared by God and the Messiah (Rev. 22:1). Other texts speak about a single kingdom that belongs to God and to the Messiah (Eph. 5:5). Note that in Greek, as in Hebrew, the word usually translated as kingdom means, in the first place, the very act of ruling as king. God the Father and his Messiah share only one throne; together they are but one act of royal ruling over his people.

And here is the main point. This ruling act of the Messiah could not be correctly understood if the first Christians had placed Jesus as an intermediate being between God and his people, or between God and his creation. Here all speculation about first-century intermediate figures is useless. Jesus could not have been understood as an intermediate figure. Why? We already know: putting Jesus as an intermediate figure between God and his creation stood in contradiction with the exclusive character of God's rule, as it was understood in the past both by the Hebrew Bible and by Jesus. If the first Christians wanted to be loyal to the central core of Jesus' message about the kingdom of God, they could not introduce an intermediate creature in a ruling position between God and the rest of his creation.

They could not. Obviously the temptation was there. The books of Chronicles sometimes say that the kings of Israel were seated on God's throne over Israel (1 Chron. 29:23; 2 Chron. 9:8). However, this throne is no longer in Jerusalem, but in heaven. Of course, one could then think that Jesus is now some kind of angel, who reigns sitting on the throne of God. Probably, some tendencies of the so-called Jewish Christianity thought like this.[20] But in doing so, they became paradoxically less "Jewish" than the "orthodox" Christians because they dared to put an angel, a being different from God, in a ruling position that only suits God himself. As a matter of fact, some of these groups ended up with a very Hellenistic worldview, introducing not just one, but a long cascade of intermediate entities between God and the creation.[21]

The Letter to the Hebrews begins with the affirmation that Jesus cannot be an angel. Then the letter quotes Ps. 45:6-7, applying it to the Messiah. As it is a psalm, it is God's Word, and this means that God himself addresses his Messiah as "God." The context is again the kingdom of God, which now Jesus himself shares with the Father.

Although the Letter to the Hebrews resumes this development, the process had begun before. Being loyal to Jesus, and being loyal to the history of monotheism, the first Christians could not understand Jesus as an intermediate figure between God and creation. The kingdom is only one. The act of reigning is only one. But God and the Messiah share this sole rule. And this means that the Messiah belongs in the monotheism of God. Jesus is Lord *(kyrios)*, the same Lord of the Septuagint translation of the Old Testament. Paul expresses it very early, inserting Jesus in the Shema of Israel (1 Cor. 8:6).[22]

Now we can better understand the reasons why some great Pauline exegetes have commented on the speed of the process wherein Jesus was identified with God, and why this process took place not in a Hellenistic context but in a Jewish context. This also explains why the first Christians, while proclaiming Jesus as Lord, never thought they were leaving their traditional monotheism. On the contrary, they were in some sense being faithful to the most exclusive character of Hebrew monotheism, which does not tolerate other ruling figures besides God. The ruling act of Jesus is the same as the ruling act of God, and therefore Jesus belongs in the midst of the royal deity of God.

20. Hans-Joachim Schoeps, *Theologie und Geschichte des Judenchristentums* (Tübingen: Mohr, 1949), pp. 71-116.

21. Jean Daniélou, *Théologie du judéo-christianisme* (Tournai: Desclée, 1958).

22. Deut. 6:4 (LXX); N. T. Wright, *What Saint Paul Really Said: Was Paul of Tarsus the Real Founder of Christianity?* (Grand Rapids: Eerdmans, 1997), pp. 65-67.

V. The Cross and Redemption

When we look back from the exaltation of resurrection and we look back to the cross, we have to think again. If Jesus belongs to the monotheism of God, his whole life is now the story of God. We can say, with Tom Wright, that the story of Jesus is the story of God becoming king.[23] But the cross is part of this story. God was in the place most opposite to any idea of power and glory. God was with Jesus on the cross.

The event at the cross, then, has a radically unexpected meaning. Jesus has experienced the abandonment of God, which means that God himself has experienced the abandonment of God. God has taken upon himself the destiny of the cursed and the sinners, the destiny of all supposedly abandoned by God. There is no place nor situation that is too far away from God. This is the core of redemption: Jesus was made sin for us (2 Cor. 5:21).

In the Old Testament, God had assumed the roles of king, of master, and of warrior. This already had important consequences, because in assuming these roles God was revealing his will of enabling a people without domination. Now, on the cross, we come to the full revelation of what it really means to be king, master, or warrior. The king, master, and warrior reveals himself as a servant and a slave. There is no more radical expression of God's love for humankind (Rom. 5:8).

At the same time, the unity of God is not broken. Even to the point of extreme humiliation and death, God continues to be the only God of monotheism. In the midst of extreme abandonment, Father and Son are still the one and only God. This unity is the fellowship of the Spirit. In the difference of Father and Son, the Spirit is not only the eternal essence of God but also a personal relation between Father and Son.

This difference and unity can be seen through Jesus' earthly life. In his ministry, Jesus reveals himself as the true Son, representing as such the original mission of all of Israel. As Son, he has an intimate relation with his Father. In Jesus' earthly life, Father and Son are revealed as such because they have a relationship. In his relation with the Father, the Son is Son because he has a Father, and the Father is Father because he has a Son. Relation means difference and unity. Be-

23. N. T. Wright, *How God Became King: Getting to the Heart of the Gospels* (San Francisco: HarperOne, 2012).

cause of this unity, the life and ministry of Jesus are led by the Spirit in complete unity with the Father.

From this point of view it becomes important to emphasize, as occurs in some streams of Latin American theology, that we only know who God is through Jesus Christ. He is the same as the prologue of John tells us (John 1:18). However, Jesus not only reveals himself but also reveals himself as the Son. Upon revealing himself as the Son, he reveals to us that God is also Father. The manifestation of who God is, for this reason, does not stop in Jesus. The revelation has a relational structure, although this relational structure is not a celestial model but rather that of the incarnation.

This same structure is found in our redemption. Our separation from God as sinners is bridged by the grace of Jesus, who approaches the lost and experiences our deserved destination. Reached by Jesus, we are introduced into the very fellowship of God with God, who is the Spirit. The Spirit brings us into the relationship of the Son with the Father, which means that we are inserted into the core of God's life. As we are introduced into this relationship of the Son with the Father, we are able to cry out: "Abba, Father" (Rom. 8:15; Gal. 4:6). The Spirit adopts us as children of God, brothers and sisters of Jesus, and thus we belong to God's family.

The early "trinitarian" expressions in the New Testament[24] have their roots not only in the experiences of the churches with the Spirit, but also in the certainty that Christ's abandonment by God was never a division in God. Here again the resurrection is the proof of the unity of the Spirit. It was the Holy Spirit, in unity with Father and Son, who raised Jesus from the dead, keeping the eternal unity of the monotheistic God.[25]

The "perspective of the poor," as expressed in liberation theology, could never do justice to the essential importance of the theology of the Holy Spirit. From the point of view of the first liberation theology, the Pentecostal movements that were outside of the usual clerical controls appeared as substantially alien developments, and consequently their proponents were painted as conservatives who were linked with

24. Matt. 28:19; Luke 3:22; John 3:34-35; 14:16, 26; 15:26; 16:7, 13-15; 2 Cor. 13:14; 2 Thess. 2:13-14; 1 Pet. 1:2.

25. As a matter of fact, the New Testament ascribes the resurrection to the Son himself (John 10:17-18), to the Father (mostly, see Acts 5:30), and also to the Spirit (Rom. 1:4; 8:11).

North American imperialism. From that perspective, the first liberation theologians found it incomprehensible that the movements were actually composed of the poor whose perspective they themselves had tried to assume. These were those who were incorporated into the charismatic and Pentecostal movements. However, an adequate trinitarian theology culminates precisely in the thought of the active presence of God in his people, especially among the poorest of his people. It is precisely this presence of God in the midst of his people, and not the communitarian images in the heavens, that implies a constituent demand for equality and fraternity.[26]

VI. Beyond Subjects

Upon reaching this point, it becomes clear that we cannot understand the three divine persons as "subjects," as modern philosophy and theology tend to do. The idea of God as subject does not appear to leave room for trinitarian thought: or it affirms one unique subject in heaven, or affirms three subjects, something that approaches tritheism instead of the Trinity.[27]

When the ancient councils of the church introduced the word "person" (*hypostasis* or *prosōpon*), they never thought of it in a modern sense. For example, in the Third Council of Constantinople (681), the "monotheletists" defended the idea that in Jesus there is only one will because they tended to think that in Jesus there is only one nature. The orthodox party, on the contrary, defended the view that in Jesus there are two wills because of his two natures. In both cases, they were clear that the will was not an attribute of the one person of Jesus, but an attribute of his nature. On the contrary, the modern idea of person as subject has no doubt that the will is an attribute of the person.

If Christianity would have come to the triune image of God by means of "intermediate figures," it would be easy to think of the Trinity as a unity of three different subjects. But this idea of person as

26. A fresh perspective on Latin American Pentecostalism can be found in C. Álvarez, ed., *Pentecostalismo y liberación: Una experiencia latinoamericana* (San José, Costa Rica: Departamento Ecuménico de Investigaciones, 1992).

27. An extreme example of this is Jürgen Moltmann, *Trinität und Reich Gottes: Zur Gotteslehre* (Munich: Kaiser, 1980), pp. 187-94. Some Latin American theologians, such as Leonardo Boff, are close to Moltmann's position.

subject is not in the New Testament and it is also not what the ancient church tried to say.

What we have in the Scriptures is the image of a God who has revealed himself in his act of liberating and ruling his people. This ruling is so radical that God is also proclaimed the Creator of the whole reality. In the New Testament, the rule of God shows itself as an act of extreme and radical love, even to the point of death. After the definitive revelation of God in Jesus we can say that God is love (1 John 4:8). The act of love is the very essence of God, according to the Scriptures. God is not primarily a thing, but an act; the pure act of love.

By revealing himself as love, God has revealed personal relations in himself. Love means relationships, and these are eternal relationships. God did not begin to be love in the moment of time when we experienced loving relationships with him. God is eternal love, and this means that God is love beyond the realm of creation. The loving relations in God are eternal relations. God has revealed himself as love, and this means that God has revealed himself as that which he eternally is. Trinity is not an appearance toward the creatures, but the essence of God as love.

The words used by the ancient church (*prosōpon, hypostasis*) do not mean an isolated subject, but relations. The word *hypostasis* primarily refers to an act, the act of supporting something or somebody. The word *prosōpon* means primarily the act of looking at, and therefore the act of facing, and then a face, or the front of something. To say that in God there are persons means that in God there are three eternal relations.

God as Father has revealed himself as the eternal Source of himself, including all relations included in his pure act of love. God has revealed himself as the eternal Gift of himself to the Father. And God has revealed himself as eternal fellowship between Father and Son. As eternal Source, God is creator. As eternal Gift, God is the only redeemer of the believers. As eternal Fellowship, God is the sanctifying Spirit in us (2 Cor. 13:14).

We can conclude, then, that the doctrine of Trinity essentially belongs to the Christian image of God, having its roots in the exclusivity of God, in the way this exclusivity is understood in the Hebrew Scriptures. However, the Trinity is not principally a celestial "model" but rather the very structure of the solidarity of the unique God with his people. It is a solidarity that is inseparable from the biblical idea of an exclusive monotheism of God. Precisely because it points to solidarity, and precisely because monotheism is exclusive, trinitarian language is situated precisely in the "perspective of the poor," that which liberation theology longs for. From this perspective, God is not only the eternal Father, Creator, and Almighty who makes the sun to shine on the just and the sinners. God is also God the Son, committed unto death to the oppressed, the sinners, and all those who appear to be rejected by God. And God is also the Spirit who raised Jesus from the dead, and who lives filling his people with life and giving gifts to his people. Precisely because God is like this, so also his Holy Scriptures speak to us of him.

Further Reading

Leonardo Boff, *Trinity and Society* (Maryknoll, N.Y.: Orbis, 1988).

Miguel H. Díaz, "The Life-Giving Reality of God from Black, Latin American, and US Hispanic Theological Perspectives," in *The Cambridge Companion to the Trinity*, ed. Peter C. Phan (Cambridge: Cambridge University Press), pp. 259-73.

Antonio González, *God's Reign and the End of Empires* (Miami: Convivium, 2012).

———, *The Gospel of Faith and Justice* (Maryknoll, N.Y.: Orbis, 2005).

Veli-Matti Kärkkäinen, *The Trinity: Global Perspectives* (Louisville: Westminster John Knox, 2007).

CHAPTER 5

Learning to See Jesus with the Eyes of the Spirit: The Unlikely Prophets of God's Reign

C. ROSALEE VELLOSO EWELL

ABSTRACT

This chapter journeys through a couple of Old Testament prophets (Jeremiah and Jonah) and Paul's correspondence with the Corinthians in order to examine the implications of the doctrine of the Trinity for how we understand the prophetic role of the church today. It offers a brief overview of how the Bible has been read in Latin America and the place of the Trinity within such readings. Then it sketches the lives of two biblical prophets in order to focus on how Christians are enabled to see Jesus through the work of the Holy Spirit in the gathered community. This trinitarian work has implications not only for scriptural reading and the formulation of doctrine but also for what can be called holistic evangelism: the witness of the church in today's society in all areas of life.

> *Credo in Deum Patrem omnipotentem; Creatorem coeli et terrae.*
> *Et in Jesum Christum, Filium ejus unicum, Dominum nostrum;*
> *qui conceptus est de Spiritu Sancto, natus ex Maria virgine . . .*

> I believe in God the Father Almighty, Maker of heaven and earth.
> And in Jesus Christ his only Son our Lord;
> who was conceived by the Holy Ghost, born of the Virgin Mary . . .

Jürgen Moltmann once asked, "Why are most Christians in the West, whether they be Catholics or Protestants, really only 'monotheists' where the experience and practice of their faith is concerned? Whether God is one or triune evidently makes as little difference to the doctrine of faith as it does to ethics."[1] I would argue that not only is this the case in the West but, with some exceptions, describes an aspect of Christian faith and practice in Latin America as well.

All theologies, all scriptural interpretations, are contextual. Whether one's theology challenges consumerism in Lima or London, poverty in Dallas or Delhi, the meaning of St. Paul's Letter to the Romans in Baltimore or Brasilia – we must always keep in mind the limits of our own language and viewpoints. In 1 Cor. 13:12 Paul says, "We see through a glass dimly." "But we do see Jesus," states the author of Hebrews (Heb. 2:9). "We see through a glass dimly" – this is learning humility and knowing that we do not have God's view of things, that we do not have all the answers or the plans or necessarily the best interpretations of Scripture. Whether we are from the north or south, east or west, the Scriptures' constant reminder, made succinct in the creed's affirmation that Jesus is Lord, is that we are not lords, not little gods who seek to control with knowledge or power. Power and knowledge are only seen in the triune God and the ways in which this God has been revealed to all of creation in Jesus and through the Spirit at work in the church.

When trying to learn about the Holy Trinity and how to live as Christians, it is fundamental for us to remember that the love between the Father, Son, and Spirit offers us a framework for how to think about our own lives and our participation in the divine life. Another word for this type of living is "discipleship" – living into God's calling of God's people, both as individuals and collectively as church. This implies also exercising the prophetic voice within our contexts. That is, the prophetic voice is intimately tied to what it means to live as God's people in the world, enabled by the Spirit to be witnesses for Jesus Christ.

I. Biblical Interpretation in Latin America

As in any other continent or community, there is no one single way the Bible is read and interpreted in Latin America. Rather, scriptural read-

---

1. Jürgen Moltmann, *The Trinity and the Kingdom: The Doctrine of God* (London: SCM, 1981), p. 1.

ings look more like the colors of a kaleidoscope, changing and shifting according to the many contexts and situations in which the Bible is read. Despite this variety, a couple of general themes have emerged over the past four decades that shed light on the theologies of the doctrine of the Trinity in this vast continent.

First, it is important to note the distinction between the theology of liberation and the Latin American Bible movement.[2] The latter refers to the changes in Bible reading at the popular level, in base ecclesial communities and among the poorest of the poor. The former is the academic, second-order reflection on some of the practices of the base communities and in conversation with key conciliar documents and Western theologies. Precisely because it is more academic, liberation theology is more well known in the West in both Catholic and Protestant circles. What is unique about the Bible movement is that it did not simply offer alternate theological formulations on old themes or different reflections on key dogmas of the church. Rather, it changed the way the Bible was read by placing the reality, that is, the social and economic problems and the oppression of the poor, in the very center. This brought the world of the Bible into the present — a "fluid transition between past and present" that illuminated "the present by considering the manifestations of God in the past."[3] In a similar way, Baptist theologian James McClendon argued that this way of reading the Bible has characterized particular communities throughout Christian history, from Peter's sermon in Acts 3 to African American spirituals of the nineteenth and twentieth centuries. It is what McClendon called the Baptist vision, "this is that, then is now" — a way of appropriating the biblical texts such that not only do they become a reality for the readers, but they also exercise their prophetic voice on those who read them.[4]

---

2. Paulo Nogueira. "Exodus in Latin America," in *The Oxford Handbook of the Reception History of the Bible*, ed. Michael Lieb et al. (Oxford: Oxford University Press, 2011), pp. 447-52.

3. Nogueira, "Exodus in Latin America," p. 448.

4. "So the vision can be expressed as a hermeneutical motto, which is shared awareness of *the present Christian community as the primitive community and the eschatological community.* In other words, the church now is the primitive church and the church on the day of judgment is the church now; the obedience and the liberty of the followers of Jesus of Nazareth is *our* liberty, *our* obedience." James Wm. McClendon Jr., *Systematic Theology*, vol. 1, *Ethics* (Nashville: Abingdon, 1986), p. 31.

Second, the theologies of Latin America reflect both the political and the ecclesial divisions in the continent. For most of the second half of the twentieth century, Latin American countries were governed by military dictatorships. At the same time Communism and the Cold War played into the psyches of Christians, especially Protestants, who were greatly influenced by conservative missionaries from North America and Western Europe, with the result that too often nothing was done to oppose the dictators and the many abuses of the political system. One could argue that during those decades the prophetic voice of the church was largely silenced and that theology and biblical interpretation emphasized spiritual transformation and the desire to get to heaven, thus paying little or no attention to what was going on in society. Of course, there were exceptions – individuals and communities that opposed such spiritualizing of the texts – but these were not the dominant voices within Christian circles. The doctrine of the Trinity was an academic discipline, ignored in practice, if not in speech, by most congregations.

Even if not always acknowledged, it was the changes in the Roman Catholic Church after Vatican II – voices and scriptural readings coming from the margins of society – that challenged the status quo and led to what today is known as "holistic" or "integral" mission movements in Latin America. This theology, aided by voices such as John Stott, Samuel Escobar, and Orlando Costas, sought to bring together the evangelical passion for evangelism with social justice practices. While this movement has been largely Christocentric, there have been some theologians and pastors articulating a more robust doctrine of the Trinity. Among such voices, Leonardo Boff is probably the most famous.

Boff, a Brazilian Catholic theologian, reminds us that when speaking of the Trinity we need to recover the proper language, the grammar of our faith – language that is specific to theological discourse and that has been battled over, debated, and fine-tuned over the centuries. At the same time, we must recognize the limitations of our language and affirm the ongoing work of the Trinity in our daily lives. As Boff puts it, if we divorce the Trinity from life, we have given up on justice, peace, love, and salvation.

> The Trinity has to do with the lives of each of us, our daily experiences, our struggles to follow our conscience, our love and joy, our bearing the sufferings of the world and the tragedies of human

existence; it also has to do with the struggle against social injustice, with efforts at building a more humane form of society, with the sacrifices and martyrdoms that these endeavors often bring. If we fail to include the Trinity in our personal and social odyssey, we have failed to show the saving mystery, failed in evangelization.[5]

Boff argues that the revelation of God as Trinity happened in the life of Jesus and the work of the Spirit in the community. This does not mean there was no previous communication of the Trinity, "because any true revelation of God's self must be Trinitarian."[6] What is new and unique in Christian theology and in our language of the Trinity is that now God has not just revealed himself to us but has communicated in person. Through Jesus of Nazareth and the Spirit at Pentecost, God takes on human history as God's own and dwells among us in our dwelling place. Yet this emphasis on history as it relates to the doctrine of the Trinity has rarely emphasized the prophetic role and the Spirit's work in the church.

II. Bible, Narratives, and Prophets

Biblical theology in Latin America has often been done in reaction to emphases or major themes coming from the North. In evangelical circles it was done either in reaction to the Roman Catholic majority or in the context of huge numerical growth but little spiritual depth, or both. There is certainly something to be learned from the West, but the danger is that it has led to a neglect of the biblical narratives, allowing the academy to set the tone of doctrinal discussions rather than letting readings of the texts shape and transform lives. The academy is not a place for prophets. Their voices are dampened or dismissed as yet one more interesting idea. It is the reminder of the connection between the Trinity and social justice, and between the Trinity and the politics of God's reign, that is perhaps the greatest inheritance of Latin American trinitarian theology. And if Boff is correct about the implications of the Trinity for daily life, then we must learn to listen to the prophetic voices.

Perhaps Jeremiah and Jonah are unlikely candidates for a discus-

5. Leonardo Boff, *Trinity and Society* (Maryknoll, N.Y.: Orbis, 1988), p. 157.
6. Boff, *Trinity and Society*, p. 10.

sion about the Trinity. While one cannot cite passages in these books where the triune God is made evident, the narratives themselves and the stories of these men illustrate Boff's point about the ways the Trinity interacts with our understanding of God's call on each of us to work toward justice and salvation in ways that very well might lead to suffering and martyrdom. Furthermore, Jeremiah and Jonah illustrate a kind of obedience (even if they do so begrudgingly) that God demands of God's people and the implied politics of being a faithful community. Being faithful to God's call results in participation in the divine plan for the redemption of all of creation – participation in the life of the Trinity that is being in communion and that challenges the structures of power and politics of this world.

As the story of God's activities with creation and with a particular people within that creation, the Scriptures often contain conflicting substories. There are narratives that suggest competing ways in which God's people listen to and understand the divine calling. One such example of rival narratives is the book of Jeremiah, which recounts the final days of Israel-Judah under Assyrian domination and the bloody transition to domination under Nebuchadnezzar of Babylon. The expanse of the Babylonian Empire led to the destruction of Jerusalem, with its temple and the king's palace burned to the ground in 587 B.C.E., and most of the city's prominent citizens taken into exile. As Old Testament scholar R. E. Clements describes the state of affairs in Judah,

> At one stroke the year 587 witnessed the removal of the two institutions – the temple and the Davidic kingship – which had stood as symbolic assurances of God's election of Israel. Their loss was far greater than the loss of national prestige and left the entire understanding of Israel's special relationship to Yahweh its God in question. What happened demanded total reappraisal and rethinking of Israel's self-understanding as the People of God.[7]

Christopher Seitz suggests that Jeremiah reflects "to a greater degree than other prophetic books a situation of conflict."[8] The conflicts in

---

7. R. E. Clements, *Jeremiah,* Interpretation: A Bible Commentary for Teaching and Preaching (Atlanta: John Knox, 1988), p. 6.

8. Christopher R. Seitz, *Theology in Conflict: Reactions to the Exile in the Book of Jeremiah* (Berlin: de Gruyter, 1989), p. 2.

Jeremiah are numerous – they are within the community in Judah, within also the communities who were exiled to Babylon, and there are still conflicts in Judah after 597 and 587 B.C.E. Moreover, it is precisely the situation of exile that is the focus of the conflicts. These are the very conflicts that gave rise to the distinct tradition in the canon of what is known as the "exilic or Golah tradition."[9] Where is the revelation of God in the exile? What is unique about Jeremiah that enabled him to hear the voice of God's Spirit and to proclaim, even to his own harm, the type of obedience God demanded of God's people?

By the time of Ezra, at the end of the exilic period, the people had learned confession and repentance for the sins of idolatry and syncretism that had characterized most of Israel's life since the giving of the Torah at Sinai and the beginning of exile in Babylon. In Jeremiah we have accounts of the competing narratives of the people's response to the crisis. The remnant in Jerusalem were not able to hear God's voice through Jeremiah – the revelation of God was hidden from them as their end shows. They disappear in Egypt, in idolatry, and Jeremiah is forced to die with them.

In *Reading in Communion*, Stephen Fowl and Greg Jones use Jeremiah's story to show how the moral life must be embodied in particular practices that are shaped by such virtues as patience, hope, and faith.[10] They explain that the situation in Judah was such that it demanded an immediate response – something had to be done. On one hand there was Hananiah, the false prophet, calling the people to join Egypt in a revolt against Babylon and arguing that in doing so the Lord would bring Israel through the war and restore peace to Jerusalem. On the other hand there was Jeremiah, telling the people that subjection under Babylon would last a long time and that they needed to learn to live with it, to be faithful to God in spite of their desperate situation. He instructs them to plant gardens, build houses, marry, and so on. However, as Fowl and Jones point out, the people were not trained to hear the words of God as spoken through Jeremiah – they had not been part of faithful practices that would shape them into faithful people who would be willing to understand and obey Jeremiah's call.

Jeremiah's story does not end in 587 B.C.E. After the siege of Jerusa-

---

9. Seitz, *Theology in Conflict*, pp. 4-5.

10. Stephan E. Fowl and L. Gregory Jones, *Reading in Communion: Scripture and Ethics in Christian Life* (Grand Rapids: Eerdmans, 1991), p. 91.

lem, Judah's king Zedekiah is blinded and taken into exile. Nebuchadnezzar leaves a remnant in Judah, including Jeremiah, and Gedaliah is
made governor over the province. For a short period, it looked as though
the people would finally heed Jeremiah's call. Gedaliah attempted to
implement some of the policies suggested by Jeremiah and to follow the
prophet's words: "Fear not to serve the Chaldeans: dwell in the land,
and serve the king of Babylon, and it shall be well with you" (Jer. 40:9-
10). But this brief turn to obedience was short-lived. Led by Ishmael, a
descendant of David, the people react against Gedaliah and assassinate
him and others who had sought the welfare of the city on Jeremiah's
terms. Following Gedaliah's death, Ishmael and his cohorts rebel against
Babylon, but they are overthrown by Nebuchadnezzar with equal violence. Then, in fear of further reprisals from Babylon, the rest of the
people decide to immigrate to Egypt (Jer. 41:16-18). Once again they ask
Jeremiah for a word from God, but again he tells them words they are
not prepared to hear. He tells them not to go to Egypt but to remain in
the land, where they will prosper. For his pronouncements against Israel's unfaithfulness and against Israel's kings and its warfare, Jeremiah
is mocked, imprisoned, and suspected of treason. The people reject his
word and turn toward Egypt. And, as Karl Barth so poignantly puts it,

> [So Israel] returned to the place from which Yahweh has once called
> and led their fathers by the word of Moses. The difference is that
> this time the prophet does not lead. . . . And so they disappear and
> Jeremiah with them. They for their part are given the lie by events.
> And he is silenced by them as he had been all his life.[11]

Jeremiah had the eyes of the Spirit of God to see and to know the type
of obedience God demanded of his people and the particular ways God
invited the people to participate in God's liberation of them. But the
political implications of Jeremiah's prophetic vision included the loss
of power, the submission to foreign domination, and the work toward
justice at the local, community level. This was not the kind of God the
people wanted to obey.

The story of Jonah highlights the politics of Trinity, though again,
one would have to do some serious exegetical acrobatics to come up

---

11. Karl Barth, *Church Dogmatics,* ed. Geoffrey W. Bromiley and T. F. Torrance,
trans. Geoffrey W. Bromiley (Edinburgh: T&T Clark, 1958), IV/1, p. 474.

with Father, Son, and Holy Spirit in the four short chapters of the book of Jonah. That is not the point. Rather, the narrative tells us that the word of the Lord came to Jonah and told him to go to Nineveh, the seat of power of a cruel and ruthless force in the region, and to tell them to repent or face destruction. Nineveh was the capital of the Assyrian Empire, which was already past its peak when this story was told. It was failing and was plagued by internal corruption and mismanagement. Assur was its god — a violent, cruel, and dominating god, a god who stands in stark contrast to the loving, liberating, covenantal God of Israel. What person in their right mind would want to face Assur?

Jonah is the liberation theologian of his time. He comes from the margins, he is oppressed, his people are suffering, and he is trying to listen to God, to reveal God to his people. So when God says, go to Nineveh, it is like saying, "Don't bother with the margins right now — I want you to go to those in power so that I might redeem them." It is easier to be Nahum and to predict the fall of empire than to preach its salvation. Jonah has his own prejudices and is a grumpy character. But despite his unwillingness, he does not lose the vision of what God demands of him. He also does not lose his courage and finally submits to participating in God's work, even if it means forfeiting his own life at the hands of the enemy.

Victorio Araya argues that faith "in the liberator God of the poor is the profession that God *alone* is liberator in the authentic sense of the word."[12] But how is God liberator? Araya asks, and he answers by suggesting that human beings participate in God's redemptive activities in creation "*from beneath* . . . the God of the Bible is a God with a commitment to human history, a God who assumes the risks of the option for the poor, who remains faithful to the task of re-creating life, and who thus invites us to enter into alliance, a covenant to transform the world by humanizing life."[13]

Jonah and Jeremiah have the eyes to see what God is doing and the link between God's revelation to them — which Boff would say is trinitarian, even if the prophets did not articulate it as such — and their participation in God's mission in creation. Being obedient entails participating in the liberating work of God as God is revealed in history.

---

12. Victorio Araya, *God of the Poor: The Mystery of God in Latin American Liberation Theology* (Maryknoll, N.Y.: Orbis, 1987), p. 149.

13. Araya. *God of the Poor*, p. 150.

The danger in many articulations of the doctrine of the Trinity is that they too quickly skip over the biblical stories, making the narratives only secondary to the real agenda. The lesson from liberation theology and the Bible movement in Latin America is precisely this return to the texts, to the stories of Jeremiah and Jonah and so many others, and in making these texts part of our story today. It means learning that the same Spirit who inspired the prophets is at work in the church today and enables the church to have that prophetic voice in whatever context she finds herself.

III. Having the Eyes to See the Trinity

Again with Boff, God as Trinity is revealed fully in Jesus and at Pentecost. But in our classrooms and sermons, what Jesus are we teaching? In Latin America there are many faces, many types of Jesus — from the revolutionary Che Guevara to the cute, white, plump little baby in Mother Mary's arms. The doctrine of the Trinity demands that we learn to see Jesus with the eyes of the Spirit so that our own prejudices and politics do not blind us to the obedience to which the Father calls all his people.

How do we discern Jesus, the first-century manual laborer from Palestine, when we see through a glass dimly? The church at Corinth suffered from the same self-absorption and prejudices as did Jeremiah or Jonah. The manifestations of the Spirit in that congregation — dramatic by comparison to most Sunday services — did not automatically make them more holy or wise. And yet, despite the limitations and sin of the Corinthians, the triune God was made real within that community. How? Why? Part of the answer lies in the fact that God is a missionary God and that the Spirit enables God's prophets to bear messages that relate directly to the people's witness, whatever their context. As Chris Wright observes, "God sent his prophets to expose the wickedness of his people and to warn them of its dire consequences . . . the major features of the message of those earlier prophets, sent by God's Spirit, were the fundamental requirements of God's law: to do justice, to show mercy and compassion, and to reject the exploitation of the needy . . . the prophetic Spirit of *truth* is also the Spirit of *justice*."[14] These themes of justice

14. Christopher J. H. Wright. *Knowing the Holy Spirit through the Old Testament* (Downers Grove, Ill.: IVP Academic, 2006), pp. 82-83.

and truth are the ones Paul takes on when writing to Corinth. Though the particularity of the issues of that Gentile congregation might be different from those of the people living at the time of Jeremiah or Jonah, the call to be God's faithful people remains the same. This call has everything to do with our participation in the triune life of God.

Father, Son, and Holy Spirit exist in perpetual relationship. John Baxter-Brown notes that "it is an energetic and dynamic relationship that inevitably is centrifugal in that it is outward looking. The metaphor is not exact, but it suffices here in that the very act of creation displays a fundamental aspect of God's nature: God is missionary. The creative urge, also given to all life, is to create something new whether it be a baby or a piece of art. So it must be with God's people in community: the creative urge is the basis for mission and evangelism, to see God re-create humanity one story at a time."[15] The metaphor of new birth is very apt, for God is both Creator and Re-creator. If the church is to see Jesus with the eyes of the Spirit and embody the prophetic call to justice and truth, then in such living we reflect something of God's creative nature, and we too will be missionary-oriented. It is our calling to be caught up in the Trinity's work of redemption and new creation.

But we need equipping for this task: the Father calls, the Son commissions and shows the way, and the Spirit empowers and comforts. Baxter-Brown captures the reality well: "This can be seen in the rather muddled and messy Corinthian church as Paul highlights the missionary nature of God, embodies the prophetic role in his own ministry, and teaches about the essential nature of the Son's work, especially the central importance of his death and resurrection and the need the Corinthians had (and we have today) of God's Spirit."[16]

Paul's correspondence with the Corinthians displays the urgency of their calling – they must sort out their common life, from sexual ethics to how they share their food – so that their witness in that pagan context is one of truth and justice. Learning to see the way of Jesus with the eyes of the Spirit means learning to live as a particular community that embodies the love of the persons of the Trinity and displays this love to neighbor, whether friend or enemy.

15. John Baxter-Brown, "Evangelism through the Eyes of Jesus: Reflections on the Trinity" (unpublished notes, Salisbury, UK, 2013).
16. Baxter-Brown, "Evangelism."

Drawing on Martin Buber's *I and Thou*, Timothy Gorringe argues,

> Responding to the Thou in my neighbour is living within God, within the pattern of correspondences and relations which he calls forth and which constitute created reality. As we relate, we are in the image of God, for the image is the echoing of the relationship God is. As, and only as, we relate we live in the Spirit.
>
> That human beings exist only in community is the most obvious starting point for any anthropology, given the fact that they are formed by language, which is by definition social. . . . There have been philosophies . . . which have sought essential humanness in solitude. . . . Nevertheless, both Judaism and Christianity have in general repudiated this option, affirming community as central to human being. . . . Christianity not only affirms humanity as fellow humanity, but understands fellow humanity as the sacrament of our encounter with God. . . . Through my neighbour I know God . . . the Spirit works and is known in this encounter. . . . The one who is ultimately Other, who stubbornly resists all attempts to fit him in to a ready-made category, is Jesus of Nazareth.[17]

Gorringe is not making a particular point about the Trinity, but shows clearly that understanding our place in community is fundamental to being made part of God's life and receiving God's revelation. In his debates with the Corinthians Paul is making the same point – they must understand that how they live as a community has huge implications, in fact, life-and-death implications, for how they exist as God's people. Having the eyes of the Spirit means they see Jesus of Nazareth and live according to that revelation. If their encounters with one another are less than adequate, they not only fail to see Jesus but also fail to show Jesus to those around them – in Boff's words, they run the risk of failing at evangelization.

At the beginning of 1 Corinthians 3 Paul shows the Corinthians that their jealousy, quarreling, and many divisions are directly tied to how they live in the Spirit. Indeed, those who are not spiritual will not receive the gifts of the Spirit (1 Cor. 2:14), though Paul has already affirmed in 1:7 that they are not lacking in any spiritual gift – and how

17. Timothy J. Gorringe. *Discerning the Spirit: A Theology of Revelation* (London: SCM, 1990), pp. 74-75.

does he know this? He knows because their testimony of Christ has been strengthened in speech and knowledge (1:5-6). It is a dangerous game they are playing, and the apostle is trying his hardest to persuade them again to live lives worthy of Christ.

Like the church in Latin America (and all around the world), there are issues of power and greed that threaten to break apart the community in Corinth. Paul plays on popular conceptions of wisdom and honor to show that the ways the world conceives of such power are very different from the ways of God's Spirit, and it is with the eyes of the Spirit that they must relearn to orient their individual and their collective lives. In the history of God's dealings with creation, God has called the most unlikely people to be his voice and his instruments in a broken world. It is no different with Corinth – some might be wise, but not all, some might be powerful, but not all (12:26-31). God's Spirit rests on very unlikely and often unwilling prophets asking them to show the world what it means to follow Jesus. For Paul, the Corinthian church is in this great line of people called to challenge wisdom, strength, and might so that the world might know God's justice and be drawn into God's wisdom.

The dynamics of the narrative of 1 and 2 Corinthians and the reports of Paul's ministry in the book of Acts show both how the apostle is called to be a prophet – calling the people back to justice and truth, to living as the missionary people they are meant to be – and how those who listen to the prophet become prophets themselves. The people of God are called to be a missionary people because in so doing they participate in God's life. Such participation requires and is enabled by the Spirit, who guides and teaches so that the life of Jesus is made real in whatever context the community finds itself. In the Bible movement mentioned earlier, Jesus is not a remote rabbi from the first century, but is present in and with the sufferings of the people in poor villages in Peru or an overcrowded prison in megacities like São Paulo. Being part of the life of the triune God means witnessing to Jesus in words, deeds, and character wherever we are.

Latin American theologians, from the Catholic Boff to the Methodist Miguéz Bonino, have gifted the church with an emphasis of God as Trinity at work in the community. Furthermore, they remind us that this community has been called to be a prophetic voice, a voice for justice and peace, and that such justice cannot be divorced from the life and teachings of Jesus. Insofar as we listen to the Spirit, we are able to see Jesus even in the least of these, and to embody in our relationships the obedience to the Father that has called us to himself through the Son and the Spirit.

Further Reading

Victorio Araya, *God of the Poor* (Maryknoll, N.Y.: Orbis, 1987).

Leonardo Boff, *Holy Trinity, Perfect Community* (Maryknoll, N.Y.: Orbis, 2000).

———, *Trinity and Society* (Maryknoll, N.Y.: Orbis, 1998).

José Miguéz Bonino, *Faces of Latin American Protestantism* (Grand Rapids: Eerdmans, 1997).

Orlando E. Costas, *Liberating News: A Theology of Contextual Evangelization* (Eugene, Ore.: Wipf & Stock, 2002).

Timothy J. Gorringe, *Discerning the Spirit: A Theology of Revelation* (London: SCM, 1990).

Veli-Matti Kärkkäinen, *The Trinity: Global Perspectives* (Louisville: Westminster John Knox, 2007).

CHAPTER 6

Asian Reformulations of the Trinity: An Evaluation

NATEE TANCHANPONGS

ABSTRACT

This essay looks to advance the way evangelicals do theology in context by examining proposals by four Asian theologians (Raimundo Panikkar – Indian, Jung Young Lee – Korean, Brahmabandhab Upadhyaya – Indian, and Nozomu Miyahira – Japanese) in their usage of indigenous resources to help reformulate the doctrine of the Trinity. After presenting overviews of these proposals, they are evaluated for biblical authenticity in light of an evangelical framework. The measuring stick used for assessing these proposals is the context-to-text model, which puts forward that a commitment to the primacy of the Bible and an affirmation of the turns to the interpreter's context can coexist only if there is a movement or transformation from context to the text. This model requires elements in the interpreter's context to be dynamic, nonnormative, and modifiable. Out of this context-to-text paradigm, two evaluative criteria will be suggested.

Introduction

In the article "One Rule to Rule Them All," Kevin Vanhoozer assesses the modern approach to biblical interpretation.[1] Modernity had

1. Kevin Vanhoozer, "One Rule to Rule Them All? Theological Method in an Era of

searched for the one objective method to rule over the subjectivity of the interpreters. With this failed attempt, postmodernity has taken three turns to the interpreter's context.[2] The first is the turn to social location, where the horizons of the interpreters are accounted for more seriously. Moreover, the reality of human situatedness shows that there can never be absolute objectivity from a human standpoint. The second is a turn to social situation, which focuses on the aim of doing theology. On this view, a social context is not only the setting for doing theology but also becomes the objective for doing theology. As such, the goal of theology is to transform society by addressing its ills.[3] Thus social context raises questions, the answers of which lead to praxis for the transformation of the social context. The third is a turn to cultural identity, where cultural contexts provide indigenous resources for doing theology. Thus a theology is contextual if it answers the questions posed by the context, and if it also uses indigenous resources and vernacular categories.

Evangelicals are making good progress with the first two hermeneutical turns to context. In the past decade or so, we have been much more aware of the interpretive turn to social location. In 2008, the Theological Commission of the World Evangelical Alliance (WEA-TC) commissioned a study unit on contextualization. What perhaps distinguishes this group from past efforts made by evangelicals is that the study unit approached contextualization, "aware of but not intimidated by postmodern and global challenges."[4] Likewise, mobilization by groups like the Micah Network has shown a relatively recent push for integral mission among evangelicals in the global context. This is a definitive turn to social situation. We now pay more attention to the injustices in Latin America, the poverty of Africa, and the human trafficking in Asia, and we may look to the Scripture's prophetic voice to speak into these problems of our social situations.

However, it is the third hermeneutical turn, to the interpreter's con-

---

World Christianity," in *Globalizing Theology: Belief and Practice in an Era of World Christianity,* ed. Craig Ott and Herold Netland (Grand Rapids: Baker Academic, 2006).

2. Vanhoozer, "One Rule to Rule Them All," pp. 92-99.

3. Vanhoozer, "One Rule to Rule Them All," p. 97.

4. Cited from Kevin Vanhoozer's recommendation on the back cover of *Local Theology for the Global Church: Principles for an Evangelical Approach of Contextualization,* ed. Matthew Cook, Rob Haskell, Ruth Julian, and Natee Tanchanpongs (Pasadena: William Carey, 2010).

text, that evangelicals tend to overlook. This turn to cultural identity, if done well, would unlock the full potential of contextualization and aid our understanding of Scripture. But the success of taking such a turn must be measured by how well we use these resources without being held captive by them.[5] As a way forward, I propose that we look at attempts by four Asian theologians in their use of indigenous resources for the reformulations of the doctrine of the Trinity: Raimundo Panikkar's cosmotheandrism, Jung Young Lee's yin-yang, Brahmabandhab Upadhyaya's *saccidananda*, and Nozomu Miyahira's betweenness-concord. I shall point out specific elements in these proposals that substantiate their hermeneutical methods and will then evaluate the legitimacy of these proposals in light of an evangelical framework.[6]

I. Some Reformulations of the Trinity in Asia

Raimundo Panikkar (India)

Raimundo Panikkar has a Spanish Roman Catholic mother and a Hindu father. He became a Catholic priest and a renowned theologian. Panikkar is a self-proclaimed pluralist who dialogued with the likes of John Hick. He desires to see peaceful coexistence and dialogue between major world religions, an intention and effort that should be commended in an age when religious violence permeates much of our world, and especially in the multireligious Asia.

In the larger picture, Panikkar looks to the doctrine of the Trinity to advance his pluralistic agenda, seeing the mystery of the Trinity as "the ultimate foundation for pluralism."[7] Vanhoozer explains this connection by distinguishing Panikkar's pluralism from the "unitive" ones. He appraises Panikkar's work, saying,

5. Natee Tanchanpongs, "Developing a Palate for Authentic Theology," in Cook, Haskell, Julian, and Tanchanpongs, *Local Theology for the Global Church*, pp. 109-23.

6. This framework will be referred to as the context-to-text model, which I will elaborate below.

7. Raimundo Panikkar, "The Jordan, the Tiber and the Ganges," in *The Myth of Christian Uniqueness: Toward a Pluralistic Theology of Religions*, ed. John Hick and Paul F. Knitter (Maryknoll, N.Y.: Orbis, 1987), p. 110. Elsewhere Panikkar makes this even more explicit. See Panikkar, *The Trinity and World Religions: Icon-Person-Mystery* (Madras: Christian Literature Society, 1970), p. 42.

Panikkar wishes to make a suprarational "cosmic confidence in reality," rather than a universal theory of religions, the basis for interreligious conversation and cooperation. Each concrete religion offers only a perspective, a window to the whole. . . . The very incommensurability of the religions is the condition for a kind of trinitarian perichoresis in which each religion is a dimension of the other, since each represents the whole of the human experience in a concrete way.[8]

This view of a "suprarational cosmic reality" is Panikkar's trinitarian reformulation, which he calls cosmotheandrism.

While at first glance it may appear that Panikkar draws on the Christian doctrine of the Trinity to help structure religious dialogues and a theology of religions, a closer study shows the contrary. Rather than applying Christian beliefs about the Trinity to a multireligious context, Panikkar uses his multireligious context to reshape traditional understandings of the Trinity. He begins building his trinitarian proposal on *advaitic* (nondualistic) Hinduism, saying that the Father and the Son are neither separate nor one in the same.[9] This neither-nor logic opens up the possibility of moving into a region of the "excluded middle," where the law of noncontradiction does not apply.

Cosmotheandrism involves the confluence of the *cosmos*, *theos*, and *andros*, which forms "the three irreducible dimensions which constitute the real."[10] There is a kind of perichoresis, "indwelling within one another," of these three dimensions of reality.[11] As a result, he sees cosmotheandrism as a trinitarian metaphysics and "the acme of a truth that permeates all realms of being and consciousness."[12] For Christians, this truth is the Trinity. Yet there also exists a generic trin-

8. Kevin Vanhoozer, "Does the Trinity Belong in a Theology of Religions?" in *The Trinity in a Pluralistic Age: Theological Essays on Culture and Religion*, ed. Kevin Vanhoozer (Grand Rapids: Eerdmans, 1997), p. 58.

9. Panikkar, *Trinity and World Religions*, p. 61.

10. Raimundo Panikkar, *The Cosmotheandric Experience: Emerging Religious Consciousness* (Maryknoll, N.Y.: Orbis, 1993), p. ix. For further discussion on this, see Jyri Komulainen, *An Emerging Cosmotheandric Religion? Raimon Panikkar's Pluralistic Theology of Religions*, Studies in Christian Mission 30 (Boston: Brill, 2005), p. 188.

11. Raimundo Panikkar, "The Myth of Pluralism: The Tower of Babel — A Meditation on Non-Violence," *Cross Current* 29, no. 2 (1979): 214.

12. Raimundo Panikkar, *The Trinity and the Religious Experience of Man* (Maryknoll, N.Y.: Orbis, 1973), p. xi.

itarian substructure in all other religions. Panikkar is convinced that this substructure is the foundational *oikoumenē* of the world faiths.

Cosmotheandrism functions as a metaphysics that enables Panikkar to realize his pluralistic vision of reality. But as he moves toward his pluralism, Panikkar must radically alter the traditional understanding of the Trinity. In the end, Panikkar's Trinity is neither three nor one — because his "trinity" is really just the Son and because it constitutes three independent (though interpenetrating) entities: *cosmos, theos,* and *andros.*

Jung Young Lee (Korea)

Jung Young Lee, a first-generation Korean American, asks, How can God be both one and three at the same time? The problem, according to Lee, is found in the Western tendency to think solely in either/or terms. As such, Lee suggests that we utilize the rich indigenous resources of Asia, specifically the yin-yang framework, to help explicate the doctrine of the Trinity.

There are four main characteristics of Lee's yin-yang logic.[13] First, yin-yang is symbolic thinking. Like Panikkar, Lee suggests that God is unknowable. While Panikkar equates the Father with silence, Lee borrows from the *Tao Te Ching,* which says that "those who know about God do not speak and those who speak about God do not really know him."[14] With this, Lee makes a clear Kantian move to introduce his symbolic thinking:

> We must recognize . . . that everything we say or attempt to say about God is not about God himself but about our perception of God through the symbols or images that are meaningful within the limits of our own existence in time and space.[15]

Lee admits that the Trinity is a symbol that points to God, but prefers to describe the Godhead through the East Asian framework of yin-yang.

13. Jung Young Lee, *The Trinity in Asian Perspective* (Nashville: Abingdon, 1996), p. 54.
14. Lee, *The Trinity in Asian Perspective,* p. 50.
15. Lee, *The Trinity in Asian Perspective,* p. 50.

Second, yin-yang is based on a both/and logic. Lee maintains that he is not trying to replace either/or reasoning, but proposes that we use both/and as a background framework that includes both both/and and either/or structures, thus making yin-yang a more holistic and inclusive approach to the knowledge of God.[16]

According to Lee, relationality is the third characteristic of yin-yang. He posits that "relationship is *a priori* to an entity," in that a given relationship determines what is yin and what is yang.[17] As such, neither yin nor yang is fixed, because something or someone could be yin in one relationship and yang in another. Relativity is thus inevitable.[18]

Finally, change is the ultimate reality in yin-yang. In the end, yin-yang is not a symbol of the beings interacting as yin and yang, but a symbol of the change in their interactions. In other words, what is fundamental to yin-yang relationship is not the being, but change. Lee borrows from the *I Ching* in referring to "change" as "the Great Ultimate," so that being is simply the manifestation of change.[19] Hence, when Lee states that yin and yang are opposites but are united in the Great Ultimate, he is saying that the process of change can integrate elements that seem conflicting or even contradictory.[20]

What looks like a union of two entities in yin-yang construction, Lee insists, is really three. The symbol of yin-yang should probably be understood as "yin in yang" and "yang in yin." Hence, Lee maintains,

> When two (or yin and yang) include and are included in each other, they create the trinitarian relationship. . . . This inclusiveness can be simply symbolized by the proposition [*sic*] 'in,' the inner connecting principle of yin and yang. . . . The Father and the Son are one in their 'inness,' but at the same time, they are three because 'in' represents the Spirit, the inner connecting principle which cannot exist by itself.[21]

---

16. Lee, *The Trinity in Asian Perspective*, pp. 34-35.

17. Lee, *The Trinity in Asian Perspective*, p. 52.

18. Lee, *The Trinity in Asian Perspective*, p. 53.

19. Lee, *The Trinity in Asian Perspective*, p. 27. Lee's theology of change and process theology are similar, with two main differences. First Lee's theology of change is cyclical, while process theology operates with a linear view. Second, process theology presupposes creativity, whereas Lee's does not (see Veli-Matti Kärkkäinen, *The Trinity: Global Perspectives* [Louisville: Westminster John Knox, 2007], p. 318).

20. Lee, *The Trinity in Asian Perspective*, p. 27.

21. Lee, *The Trinity in Asian Perspective*, p. 58.

He justifies creating threeness from duality through the *Tao Te Ching*, in which it is written, "The Tao gives birth to one. One gives birth to two. Two gives birth to three. Three gives birth to all things."[22]

With this East Asian metaphysical move, Lee claims that everything can be described in terms of yin-yang symbolism, and hence everything can be regarded as a trinitarian act.[23] Furthermore, Lee correlates the biblical concept of the Trinity with what he calls the East Asian trinitarian notion, comprising heaven as Father, earth as Mother, and humanity as their children.[24]

Brahmabandhab Upadhyaya (India)

Brahmabandhab Upadhyaya was a nineteenth-century Hindu convert to Christianity (1861-1907). As a Roman Catholic theologian who was fully committed to Thomism, Upadhyaya believed in the Christian gospel message while simultaneously subscribing to a form of natural theology that allowed him to find fragments of divine truth in other religions.[25] These fragments of truth served as a *preparatio evangelica*, upon which "the supernatural truths of scripture, which cannot be apprehended through reason, but received as revelation from God, should be grown."[26]

However, Upadhyaya was frustrated with the inability of Christianity to make headway in India, in part because many Western theological expressions were often incomprehensible to Indians. Hence, he spent his whole life looking to give Christianity local Indian understanding using the language and thought form of the Hindu philosophies.[27] Timothy Tennent praises Upadhyaya because he "earnestly

---

22. Lee, *The Trinity in Asian Perspective*, p. 62.

23. Lee, *The Trinity in Asian Perspective*, pp. 52, 63.

24. Lee, *The Trinity in Asian Perspective*, p. 63.

25. Timothy C. Tennent, *Building Christianity on Indian Foundations: The Legacy of Brahmabandhav Upadhyay* (Delhi: ISPCK, 2000), p. 12.

26. Orville De Silva, "Upadhyaya, Brahmabandhab," in *Indian Christian Thinkers*, ed. Anand Amaladass (Chennai: Satya Nilayam, 2005), p. 262.

27. Timothy C. Tennent, "Trinity and Saccidananda in the Writings of Brahmabandhav Upadhyaya," in *The Gospel among Religions: Christian Ministry, Theology, and Spirituality in a Multifaith World*, ed. David Brockman and Ruben L. F. Habito (Maryknoll, N.Y.: Orbis, 2010), p. 183.

sought to use the language of advaitic Hinduism as an interpretive bridge or hermeneutic whereby he might be able to better communicate Christianity to enquiring Hindus."[28] Upadhyaya believed he was simply doing with Hindu beliefs what Aquinas had done with Aristotelian philosophy.[29] When Christianity first met Hinduism, the Christians simply dismissed the *advaita* (nondual) Vedanta school of Hindu philosophy as a form of pantheism. On the contrary, Upadhyaya commended it as the highest point that human reason has attained in India, fit to be the starting point for his trinitarian reformulation.

Upadhyaya interacted with Sankara (788-820), the founder of the *advaita* Vedanta school, who posited that Brahman is the Ultimate Reality and therefore must be *asanga* ("Absolute") and *nirguna* ("Unrelated").[30] If this is so, Sankara reasoned, then the world cannot be real because there is no reality outside the Absolute (monistic nondualism).[31] To safeguard the doctrine of aseity, Upadhyaya agreed with Sankara, but resolved the monistic problem by making two distinctions: first, between what is necessary and what is contingent in the Brahman; and second, between the unchanging essence and the free action of Brahman's attributes. As such, creation is not an intrinsic attribute of the divine nature, and it is not necessary to his nature to create because the Brahman is self-sufficiently related *within*.[32] Upadhyaya sums up, saying, "Thus God has an eternal, necessary relationship within himself; but all relationships outside of himself are not necessary, but contingent *(vyavaharika)*."[33] To make this statement, Upadhyaya identified the Trinity with the upanishadic doctrine of Brahman as *saccidananda (Sat-Cit-Ananda)*.

Tennent states that in the later Upanishads, the Brahman is often described as *sat* ("being" or "reality"), *cit* ("intelligence" or "con-

---

28. Tennent, "Trinity and Saccidananda," p. 183.

29. *Sophia Monthly* 4, no. 7 (July 1897): 8-9. (*Sophia* was a monthly Catholic journal between January 1894 and March 1899 and became a weekly publication between June 16 and December 8, 1900).

30. Tennent, *Building Christianity on Indian Foundations*, p. 123.

31. Tennent, *Building Christianity on Indian Foundations*, p. 145.

32. Tennent, *Building Christianity on Indian Foundations*, pp. 219, 223. Upadhyaya believes the Vedantic philosophers realized that God cannot go outside himself to satisfy his infinite knowledge and bliss. But rather than seeing the intratrinitarian relationship, they either deny reality external to God or see reality as a part of God.

33. *Sophia Monthly* 4, no. 8 (August 1897): 9.

sciousness"), and *ananda* ("bliss").[34] For Upadhyaya, strictly speaking only God can be called *sat*. Only he has absolute, eternal, immutable, and infinite self-existence. All else has contingent existence, is limited in time and space, and is always bounded by change.[35] Consequently, God's *sat* must imply *cit*, or "knowledge." As true being, God must know himself, and his self-knowledge is expressed in an inward word or image. While our knowledge of ourselves is "accidental and transitory," God's self-knowledge is perfect. This perfect relationship is such that

> His eternal self-comprehension or word is to be conceived as identical with the divine nature and still as distinct from the Supreme Being in as far as he by comprehending himself generates His word. God, knowing himself by producing or generating His own image and word, is called Father; and God as known by himself by this inward generation of the word is called the Word or the Son.[36]

Finally, Upadhyaya identifies God the Spirit as *ananda*, or bliss. According to him, this term implies that God, who self-exists, is "self-sufficient, self-satisfied and not dependent upon any relation which is not co-terminus with his substance,"[37] because that which is "obliged to form alliance with something other than its own self cannot be essentially happy."[38]

Nozomu Miyahira (Japan)

Nozomu Miyahira wants the Scripture's understanding of the Trinity to be better understood by the Japanese. He sees the need to rearticulate the traditional Western "three persons in one substance" formulation in a vernacular category. Hence Miyahira suggests building a new formulation on the Japanese idea of "concord" and "betweenness,"

---

34. Many agree that *saccidananda* is the most complete description of the Brahman. Tennent, "Trinity and Saccidananda," p. 186.

35. Tennent, "Trinity and Saccidananda," p. 188.

36. Tennent, "Trinity and Saccidananda," p. 186. According to Tennent, this is a summary of Upadhyaya's thought written by A. Heglin, S.J.

37. *Sophia Weekly* n.s. 1 (September 1900).

38. *Sophia Monthly* 5, no. 8 (August 1898): 119.

derived from the ancient rice-growing culture. According to him, the culture of the rice-growing community of Japan produced a way of life that centers on the concepts of *ningen* ("humanity") and *wa* ("concord"). Rice-growing agriculture at that time was labor intensive, requiring a high degree of cooperation. This setting, therefore, produced an ethos of solidarity and concord, which has become definitive in the Japanese understanding of humanity and community.[39] In the historico-etymological study of the word *ningen*, Miyahira refers to Watsuji Tetsuro, who claims that in Japanese context, humans are viewed not just as individual beings but also as beings living "between" others.[40] Thus "*ningen* can mean a human or humans in the community and these two aspects are united in the dialectic relation."[41]

Miyahira explains this further by citing Kimura Bin, who points out that "a self becomes aware of itself when it meets what is not itself."[42] This reality shows up in the Japanese language. While Western languages tend to have only one first-person pronoun, Japanese has more than ten. According to him, this is because "in Japan the self is determined by its relationship with others and is sometimes absorbed into that relationship."[43] Along the same line, according to Hamaguchi Eshun, in Japan "people are highly conscious of their situation or context, and within which they maintain an outside-in perspective."[44]

With this Japanese cultural background, Miyahira begins his reformulation of the Trinity as "three betweennesses and one concord." "Betweenness," as Miyahira presents it, is a specific kind of relationality. A typical theological discussion on relationality today tends to either talk about a general kind of relationality in the Trinity (e.g., "three persons in relation") or focus on relations between a given pair of the trinitarian members (e.g., Father-Son). Betweenness, however, always involves all three persons of the Trinity. He gives an example of the betweenness that involves the Spirit between the Father and the Son. He writes, "[The] distinctiveness of the Holy Spirit — expressed in the

---

39. Nozomu Miyahira. *Towards a Theology of the Concord of God: A Japanese Perspective on the Trinity* (Carlisle, U.K.: Paternoster, 2000), pp. 112-13.
40. Miyahira, *Towards a Theology of the Concord of God*, p. 114.
41. Miyahira, *Towards a Theology of the Concord of God*, p. 115.
42. Miyahira, *Towards a Theology of the Concord of God*, p. 115.
43. Miyahira, *Towards a Theology of the Concord of God*, p. 117.
44. Miyahira, *Towards a Theology of the Concord of God*, p. 124.

notion of 'procession' – is contrasted with the relationship between the Father and the Son characterised by begetting."[45]

Therefore there are three betweennesses in the Trinity. The first is the Father having the differentiating function of sending the Son and the Holy Spirit, albeit in different ways. Here the Father is between the begotten and the processed. The second is the Son having the differentiating function of sending the Holy Spirit from the Father (John 15:26). Here the Son is between the processor and the processed. The third is the Holy Spirit having the differentiating function of life-giver (Luke 1:35; John 6:63). Here the Holy Spirit is between the begetter and the begotten.

II. On Evaluative Criteria for Biblical Authenticity

We must now define criteria to assess these proposals for biblical authenticity. Elsewhere I have critiqued essentialist and structuralist approaches to identify syncretism.[46] Essentialist views focus on preserving the "essentials" of the gospel from being contaminated by cultural or religious contexts. Structuralist approaches define syncretism as a mixing of two or more systems, resulting in inappropriate adaptations, replacements of elements in one system by elements of another. I will not repeat my arguments in full here, but will note that if we were to use the essentialist criterion, all four reformulations would be deemed syncretistic, because they have altered, to some degree, an essential teaching of Christianity. And if we were to use the structuralist criterion, we could not tell which proposals were syncretistic, because the rules for "inappropriateness" are not spelled out.

Given these limitations, I want to propose what I have called above a context-to-text approach to guide our evaluation for biblical authenticity. A commitment to the primacy of the Bible and an affirmation of the turns to the interpreter's context can coexist only if there is a movement or transformation from context to the text. This model requires elements in the interpreter's context to be dynamic, nonnormative, and modifiable.

Furthermore, the context-to-text model parallels the reality of

45. Miyahira, *Towards a Theology of the Concord of God*, p. 148.
46. Tanchanpongs, "Developing a Palate for Authentic Theology."

sanctification. In both cases, we always begin from "who we are." In sanctification, we progress in our holiness from who we are as sinners saved by grace. Likewise, our knowledge of Scripture is always mediated through "who we are" and the things that are already a part of us.[47] This "who we are" includes our indigenous cultural elements. We utilize cultural, religious, and other vernacular concepts embedded in the language as instruments for interacting with and discovering God's Word. In both cases, "who we are" is affected by sin and is in need of transformation. It is true that we *cannot be* who we are not, but because of sin we must also *become* who we are not. Thus "who we are" requires a transformation through the work of dual agency. On the one hand, only the Holy Spirit can sovereignly sanctify us toward holy living as marked out by Scripture, and only he can illuminate and transform our minds toward Scripture. On the other hand, we have a responsibility to appropriately direct our lives (Phil. 2:12-13) and our theological works toward that holy living and holy message of Scripture respectively.

The context-to-text model for contextual theology and its connection with sanctification helps us set new criteria for assessing products of contextualization with regard to their biblical authenticity. In both we must ask similar evaluative questions. How do we know if our life or our theological product displays biblical authenticity? Which directions do they traverse? Are they moving toward Scripture? In Rom. 12:1-2, Paul urges Christians to be driven by God's mercy to holy living and to do so by *moving away from* conformity to the pattern of this world, and by *moving toward* God's good, pleasing, and perfect will. Thus by linking the theological enterprise to sanctification, I propose two criteria for evaluating biblical authenticity.

First, the biblical authenticity of a Christian whose life remains unchanged and unaffected by the transforming power of the gospel must be questioned. A sanctified life is one that is not held captive by one's "who we are," but moves away from it. Therefore, there is no sanctification and no biblical faith if lives remain unchanged and

---

47. This is Michael Polanyi's theory of tacit knowledge. According to him, knowledge is tacit in that there is no direct link to reality through abstract contemplation, but knowledge is always mediated through the body and the things that are already a part of us. Polanyi was a Hungarian Jew who became a Roman Catholic. He had a Ph.D. in physical chemistry, but became interested in epistemology and the critique of science's modern positivism and objectivism.

unaffected by the gospel.[48] In the same way, syncretism occurs when a product of contextualization remains captive to a conceptual scheme. As such, there is no movement away from one's contextual framework. We must ask if the Bible is transforming one's "who we are." A tell-tale sign of religious syncretism is when a Christian is identical with the society around him or her. Believers in Jesus Christ must always be reforming away from their sin-afflicted contexts. Similarly, if contextual elements used in a theological formulation remain unchanged, we might suspect some religious syncretism has occurred.

Second, if the life of a Christian does not change *toward Scripture,* there is also no biblical authenticity. The presence of change in a believer alone does not guarantee biblical authenticity, for one could change toward something else other than the Bible. Thus a sanctifying life is one that continues to embody and move *toward Scripture.* Likewise, syncretism takes place when a theological process does not direct its product toward a proper end of Scripture. Thus, if the first criterion inspects the movement away from the context of the reader, the second checks whether the movement is toward the text of Scripture.

III. Evaluation of the Trinitarian Reformulations

Panikkar's Cosmotheandrism

Panikkar's cosmotheandrism is a clear case of syncretism. There is no significant context-to-text movement of which to speak. In the end, Panikkar is caught in a vicious cycle. His theological effort traverses from his pluralist assumptions to a pluralist metaphysics, which comes back to justify his pluralist agenda. His initial objective is a pluralistic vision, which aims to create a theology of religion valid for more than one religious tradition. In a sense, cosmotheandrism is only his proof text to bring about coexistence and dialogue between the major religions. There is no movement out of his pluralistic "who he is."

In order to maintain his pluralism, Panikkar's interaction with Scripture is only notional and idiosyncratic. His pluralistic assumption dictates the meaning of Scripture by weakening the tie between Logos

---

48. This is precisely James's argument concerning authentic faith and works in James 2.

and the Spirit in order to "free" the Spirit to be present in other religions and to allow the experience of the reader to "have epistemological priority in the act of reading."[49] As such, Panikkar dehistoricizes the Bible and advances a hermeneutic that gets beyond the texts in their historical contexts to the universal realm in order to relate to diverse particularities.[50] This process makes it more convenient to read the Bible through the lens of other religions.

Lee's Yin-Yang

Lee's work clearly shows his delight in being Asian, something to be commended in an age where many of us prefer imported products, imported fashions, and imported theologies. But as I read his work, there is a sense that Lee is more concerned about showcasing his culture than talking about the Trinity from a biblical perspective. Veli-Matti Kärkkäinen warns that Lee's proposal threatens to subsume the Trinity into an Asian framework by failing to be critical of his own context.[51] Lee literally tries to force the three of the Trinity into the two of yin-yang. Kärkkäinen calls attention to the fact that "the symbolism of yin-yang − at least at the outset − represents a binitarian rather than Trinitarian structure."[52]

There are many instances where traditional Christian doctrines are being reenvisioned, reinterpreted, and restated. For example, Lee affirms unflinchingly the historical heresy of patripassianism.[53] Lee explains,

> Death and resurrection are trinitarian acts because Christ was not only the Son but also the trinitarian God. The death of Jesus on the cross was the death of the Father, who was united with the Son in the Spirit. If the death of the Son was also the death of the trinitarian God, it was also the death of the Spirit as well.[54]

49. Vinoth Ramachandra, *The Recovery of Mission: Beyond the Pluralist Paradigm* (Grand Rapids: Eerdmans, 1996), p. 99.

50. Ramachandra, *Recovery of Mission*, p. 99.

51. Kärkkäinen, *The Trinity*, p. 331.

52. Kärkkäinen, *The Trinity*, p. 332.

53. Lee, *The Trinity in Asian Perspective*, pp. 91-94.

54. Lee, *The Trinity in Asian Perspective*, p. 82. Kärkkäinen sums up Lee's heterodox teaching by saying, "The mutuality and interdependency of [yin-yang] symbolism ex-

Kärkkäinen continues to point out more unorthodox elements in Lee's proposal. For Lee, the Spirit is both personal and impersonal. Lee justifies this conclusion from a word study of *ruach*, as "wind" (the impersonal aspect) and "breath" (the personal aspect).[55] As such, Lee identifies the Spirit with *ch'i*, which is the vital, creative energy, "mother earth," and the essence of life and all existence.[56] At this point Lee exposes his pantheistic stance, saying,

> Because of the Spirit as ch'i, everything that exists is creative and alive. It is, therefore, impossible to separate spirit from matter. In other words, spirit is inseparable from matter, for they are essentially one but have two modes of existence. Because they are inseparable, thinking of matter alone without spirit or spirit alone without matter is illusory.[57]

There are many more examples of Lee's subsuming elements of trinitarian doctrine under the East Asian concept of yin-yang, such as the puzzling idea that Jesus is both male and female,[58] the contradictory notion that God is both personal and impersonal,[59] and the process theological idea that the incarnation is the perfect expression of change.[60] At root is Lee's handling of Scripture. He reinterprets many biblical passages through allegories and various symbol, word, and number games.

For example, concerning the Holy Spirit in the birth narrative of Luke 1, Lee suggests that the conception of Jesus involves two powers – the Holy Spirit and the Most High – and goes on to say that "the familial symbols of the Trinity are definitely established in this story: the Most High as the father, the Holy Spirit as the mother, and Jesus to be born as the son."[61]

Lee resorts to an allegorical reading of the manger as he tries to

---

cludes the idea of the immunity of one member of the Trinity (Father) to the experiences of the other (Son). Therefore, Lee is not critical of patripassianism, the idea of God suffering, which was deemed heretical." Kärkkäinen, *The Trinity*, p. 325.

55. Lee, *The Trinity in Asian Perspective*, pp. 96-97.
56. Kärkkäinen, *The Trinity*, p. 326.
57. Lee, *The Trinity in Asian Perspective*, p. 98.
58. Lee, *The Trinity in Asian Perspective*, pp. 78-82.
59. Kärkkäinen, *The Trinity*, p. 319.
60. Lee, *The Trinity in Asian Perspective*, p. 71.
61. Lee, *The Trinity in Asian Perspective*, p. 74.

find support for his cosmo-anthropological view of yin-yang. Lee imagines on, saying,

> Jesus in the manger does not belong to human society alone: He also belongs to the animal world of the cosmic order. . . . Thus, Jesus empties himself to fill the manger, and become the lowest form in order to unite both the human and animal worlds.[62]

For Lee, death is no longer the ultimate enemy, as Scripture strongly affirms, but it is an integral part of the dialectic of yin-yang.[63]

On the whole, Lee is less concerned about using yin-yang to help clarify and safeguard the integrity of the Bible than he is to use the Bible to proof text and preserve the meaning of yin-yang. Lee's trinitarian reformulation may be less radical than that of Panikkar, but they share similar traits. In their encounter with Scripture, they never move out of their context. For Panikkar, it is his pluralistic assumption that dictates his hermeneutics. For Lee, it is his East Asian yin-yang philosophy. Both theologians see their interpretive contexts as more fundamental, more vital, and they thus become the agendas that drive their reformulations of the doctrine. Both proposals have weak biblical foundations and are radical revisions of theological tradition, with strong pluralistic orientation.[64]

Upadhyaya's Saccidananda

Panikkar's and Lee's proposals fail the epistemic dependency criterion, and their reformulations of the Trinity remain captive to their respective conceptual schemes. Upadhyaya also uses indigenous resources, yet he allows the "text" to transform them where necessary. Upadhyaya is selective about the concepts he employs. For instance,

---

62. Lee, *The Trinity in Asian Perspective*, p. 75.

63. To this end, Lee writes, "From the cosmo-anthropological perspective, death is inseparable from life, just as life cannot exist independently from death. Life and death are neither enemies to each other nor independent, separable events." Lee, *The Trinity in Asian Perspective*, p. 83.

64. Robert Letham and Veli-Matti Kärkkäinen, "Trinity, Triune God," in *Global Dictionary of Theology*, ed. William A. Dyrness and Veli-Matti Kärkkäinen (Downers Grove, Ill.: IVP Academic, 2008), p. 911.

concerning the view of ultimate reality, there are two main schools of thought in Hinduism. *Advaita* Vedantism, a monistic nondualism, advances the view that the world is not real, because there is no reality outside the Brahman. Visistadvaita Vedantism, a form of pantheism, believes that the world is a part of the Brahman. Upadhyaya has to choose between these philosophical stances, neither of which meets the standard of Christian orthodoxy. All things considered, Upadhyaya sees pantheism as a more immediate threat.[65] In contrast, advaitism offers a view of God as the Absolute, something that resembles the doctrine of divine aseity in Thomism. As such, Upadhyaya opts for the *advaita* school as the starting point for his trinitarian reformulation.

Nevertheless, Upadhyaya must contend with the monistic nondualism. As we have seen earlier, Upadhyaya resolves this problem by first making distinctions in the Brahman between necessary and contingent and between unchanging essences and free attributes before he goes on to explicate the Brahman as *sat, cit,* and *ananda*. In effect, Upadhyaya has masterfully used the power of discourse to transform the meaning of the Brahman, hence making a context-to-text movement.

Even with this masterpiece, there are two caveats. First, the Hindu philosophy Upadhyaya has chosen as a starting point does not represent the interpretive context of most Indians. He has engaged with intellectual Hindus to win them over to the Catholic faith using "rationalist theism"[66] and has been sharply criticized for being "incomprehensible even to the most learned of Indians" and developing a theology "based on a misguided intellectualism."[67]

Beyond the choice of interpretive context, there is also a second problem: his immediate theological destination is also less than ideal. Upadhyaya, as an ardent Roman Catholic, is concerned about upholding the teachings of his church. Therefore in the best case, biblical integrity can be achieved inasmuch as Thomistic doctrines are biblical. Space does not allow us to elaborate further on this point. Suffice to say that this is a caution against primarily contextualizing a theological tradition as opposed to the Scripture itself.

65. Tennent, *Building Christianity on Indian Foundations*, pp. 220-21.

66. Orville De Silva, "Upadhyaya, Brahmabandhab," in *Indian Christian Thinkers*, ed. Anand Amaladass (Chennai: Satya Nilayam, 2005), p. 262.

67. Madhusudhan Rao, "Lessons from India: Brahmabandhab Upadhyaya and the Failure of Hindu Christianity," *International Journal of Frontier Mission* 18, no. 1 (Spring 2001): 197.

Miyahira's Betweenness and Concord

Among the four reformulations, Miyahira's proposal is most promising in light of our context-to-text criteria. He effectively affirms this scheme when he says, "Culture informs us of the framework in which theology can be formed, but culture needs more than that, to be transformed by the exegesis of Scripture."[68] For him, the adaptation of the gospel to a particular culture must be done in such a way as not to weaken the very same gospel.[69] Like Upadhyaya, Miyahira begins with his own cultural context and at once uses the linguistic power of discourse to transform and traverse the cultural elements toward the text.[70] But unlike Upadhyaya, his cultural elements are more colloquial, taken from the everyday experience of common people. And unlike Upadhyaya, Miyahira's immediate "text" is Scripture. In his reformulation of the doctrine, Miyahira directs his attention to the Gospel of John.

Miyahira juxtaposes the Japanese concept of betweenness with the book of John, observing a trinitarian relationship based on the divine internal testimony, that the Son stands in distinct betweenness of the two witness-bearers, the Father and the Spirit.[71] Similarly, he sees the concept of concord in John as the unifying relationship of the triune God, a relationship based on knowing, entrusting, and glorifying. First, the Son knows the Father because there is unity between them. No one is fit to be the eyewitness to the Father except the Son, who has close fellowship with the Father.[72] Furthermore, the Father also knows the Son because there is mutual indwelling between the Father and the Son.[73]

Second, the knowing in the Trinity leads to mutual entrusting. In this, the Son does all the redemptive work that the Father entrusts to him. The Father also entrusts all things to the Son, such as authority over all people, authority to execute judgment, and authority to give eternal life, so that the Son may complete the Father's work.[74]

Third, the entrusting relationship leads to glorification by mutual

---

68. Miyahira, *Towards a Theology of the Concord of God*, p. 4.

69. Miyahira, *Towards a Theology of the Concord of God*, p. 177.

70. An example critique of his own culture is found in Miyahira, *Towards a Theology of the Concord of God*, p. 201.

71. Miyahira, *Towards a Theology of the Concord of God*, p. 177.

72. Miyahira, *Towards a Theology of the Concord of God*, p. 178.

73. Miyahira, *Towards a Theology of the Concord of God*, p. 179.

74. Miyahira, *Towards a Theology of the Concord of God*, pp. 179-80.

manifesting and honoring. Jesus glorifies the Father by manifesting the Father in his earthly work by fulfilling it, and Jesus honors the Father by doing this work "in absolute obedience to the Father's will."[75] This mutual glorification on earth is rooted in the eternal mutual glorification of the Trinity.[76]

Miyahira explains that this three-pronged unifying concord is motivated by divine eternal love, saying, "The 'concord' as found in the active knowing, entrusting and glorifying is inseparably intertwined with the mutual love between the Father and the Son."[77]

What about the Holy Spirit? Miyahira admits that the Holy Spirit does not appear in John as much as the Father and the Son. Yet he points out that the Holy Spirit is called "another advocate," which connects him with the Son as an advocate. Specifically, Miyahira writes, "After the Son departs, the Holy Spirit as the witness to the Son will guide the disciples into all the truth by not speaking on his own, as the Son does nothing on his own, but speaking whatever he hears."[78] In this trinitarian mutuality, Miyahira argues, the Holy Spirit is also found in the knowing, entrusting, and glorifying relationship with the Father and the Son.

Conclusion

In this essay, I have tried to address both material and formal aspects of contextual theology. Materially, I have surveyed four Asian theologians' reformulations of the doctrine of the Trinity and evaluated them for biblical authenticity. On the one hand, Panikkar's cosmotheandrism and Lee's yin-yang have been found wanting. They are undeniably syncretistic because they encounter the problem of epistemic dependency; that is, the message of the Scripture has not been allowed to speak its prophetic voice into the cultures. On the other hand, Upadhyaya's *saccidananda* and Miyahira's betweenness-concord show more potential. They take cultural contexts seriously, but at the same time only assign ministerial importance to interpretive contexts. While we cannot dismiss Upadhyaya for not having a high view of Scripture, his

---

75. Miyahira, *Towards a Theology of the Concord of God*, p. 181.
76. Miyahira, *Towards a Theology of the Concord of God*, p. 181.
77. Miyahira, *Towards a Theology of the Concord of God*, p. 182.
78. Miyahira, *Towards a Theology of the Concord of God*, p. 184.

theological reformulation is immediately more concerned with preserving and communicating Thomistic doctrine. Miyahira in contrast is much more conscientious about engaging directly with the Scripture. In the end, both Upadhyaya and Miyahira can help guide us to increasingly use indigenous resources and vernacular categories in our theological enterprise.

Second, I have used the material aspects of this essay to suggest a way of doing theology in context. Evangelical contextual theology must consist of a movement from one's interpretive context toward the canonically anchored text. But how do we know that we are traversing rightly toward Scripture? In the end, biblical authenticity can be verified only in ongoing catholic dialogue. J. Nelson Jennings is right to say that "even though there are trustworthy signposts, the path down which such ongoing contextualization processes should go is not a straightforward, given matter. Nor is there any guarantee that syncretism, or contextualization gone awry, will not occur."[79] As such, doing theology in context must be done with great care, which is the impetus for our need of each other in the catholic fellowship of the Word.

Further Reading

Veli-Matti Kärkkäinen, *The Trinity: Global Perspectives* (Louisville: Westminster John Knox, 2007).

Jung Young Lee, *The Trinity in Asian Perspective* (Nashville: Abingdon, 1996).

Nozomu Miyahira, *Towards a Theology of the Concord of God: A Japanese Perspective on the Trinity* (Carlisle, U.K.: Paternoster, 2000).

Raimundo Panikkar, *The Trinity and World Religions: Icon-Person-Mystery* (Madras: Christian Literature Society, 1970).

Natee Tanchanpongs, "Developing a Palate for Authentic Theology," in *Local Theology for the Global Church: Principles for an Evangelical Approach of Contextualization*, ed. Matthew Cook, Rob Haskell, Ruth Julian, and Natee Tanchanpongs (Pasadena, Calif.: William Carey Library, 2010).

Timothy C. Tennent, *Building Christianity on Indian Foundations: The Legacy of Brahmabandhav Upadhyay* (Delhi: ISPCK, 2000).

---

79. J. Nelson Jennings, "Suburban Evangelical Individualism: Syncretism or Contextualization?" in *Contextualization and Syncretism: Navigating Cultural Currents*, ed. Gailyn Van Rheenen (Pasadena, Calif.: William Carey Library, 2006), p. 175.

CHAPTER 7

Motherliness of God: A Search for Maternal Aspects in Paul's Theology

Atsuhiro Asano

"Not at all. What the Japanese of that time believed in was not our God. It was their own gods."

(Ferreira in *Silence*)[1]

ABSTRACT

The creedal confessions begin with "We believe in God the Father." The emphasis of the metaphor of "father" in negligence of "mother" sometimes delivers the wrong message that Christianity is patriarchal. Missionary work with such a message has hindered the furtherance of the gospel, especially in so-called maternal societies. Such societies expect the members to relate to others including gods in the way a mother relates to her children. Therefore, a god with paternal dealings is not enthusiastically welcome. Yet the hindrance is a chance to read the Bible with an ear more attentive to motherly voices in it. This author, who is located in a "maternal society," reads the Epistle to the Galatians, written by one often criticized as a "chauvinist," to see if the God of Christian Scripture is exclusively patriarchal. My contention is that Paul reflects the motherliness of God in his vision for nurturing the community.

1. Shusaku Endo, *Silence*, trans. William Johnston (Rutland *et al.*: Tuttle, 1969), pp. 237-38.

I. Maternal Culture and a View of God

Silence and Motherliness of God

In his historical novel *Silence,* the Japanese Catholic author Shusaku Endo depicts the life of a Jesuit missionary, Sebastian Rodrigues, in the heat of the nationwide persecution against Christianity in the *Edo* era (1603-1867) of Japan. After some years of missionary work, he is caught and imprisoned with his flock of believers. Ferreira, an ex-Catholic missionary now apostate, is brought in by the local officials to persuade Rodrigues to renounce his faith in order to save the lives of the Japanese believers who are being tortured in prison. Rodrigues claims that he cannot abandon his God, whose merciful hand is evident on the lives of the native believers. To this Ferreira replies that the people never once believed in the Christian God but sought in God someone else. Later, Rodrigues hears this someone else's voice in prison, revealing himself as Christ, who forgives and lives alongside even those who yield to pressure to deny him. Rodrigues finally announces his apostasy but with his fellow apostate believers secretly seeks after the newly found Christ, who reflects in himself someone other than "Father God."[2]

Endo elsewhere explains that this someone is "Mother God."[3] He further elaborates that, under 250 years of strict prohibition of Christianity during the *Edo* era, those secret believers called *Sempuku* – because after denying Christ they still went underground *(sempuku)* to preserve their faith and lives[4] – were healed of the memory of their betrayal and nourished not by Father God, who is ready to condemn sins, but by Mother God, who is eager to embrace sinners with all their weaknesses.[5] During this era, the victors of faith all died a martyr's death for their courageous confessions, while the apostates survived

---

2. The ending of *Silence,* thus the aftermath of Rodrigues's apostasy, is sometimes mistaken. I agree with Kasai's interpretation. Akio Kasai, *Endo Shusaku Ron* ["On Shusaku Endo"] (Tokyo: Sobunsha, 1987), pp. 153-55.

3. Shusako Endo, "Kami No Chinmoku To Ningen No Shogen" ["God's silence and human testimony"], *Fukuin To Sekai* ["Gospel and the world"] (Sept. 1966).

4. For the history and the theology of the *Sempuku,* or underground communities, see Ann H. Harrington, *Japan's Hidden Christians* (Chicago: Loyola University Press, 1993).

5. Shusako Endo, *Haha Naru Mono* ["Motherliness"] (Tokyo: Shincho, 1975), p. 55.

to preserve the Christian faith. But that faith sees in God a mother's unconditional acceptance of their failures.[6]

When Endo narrates Christian origins in other novels, he focuses on the humanity of Jesus to the exclusion of his divinity in order to focus the reader's attention on the impact of his human suffering on earth.[7] In a similar literary strategy, Endo in *Silence* describes mother-liness and fatherliness as almost antithetical to each other – either the paternal religion of Ferreira and of the rest of Western Christianity or the maternal religion of Rodrigues and of the rest of the apostate believers – in order for the reader to be shocked by the absence of maternal aspects in current Christian theology. By his rhetorical skill of exaggeration, Endo is, so to speak, suggesting that theologians, in-cluding New Testament theologians, should examine closely whether Scripture reveals something motherly about the Christian God.[8]

Maternal Longing and the Discussion of God

Where did the longing for motherliness derive from? It is not simply a theological mutation among the community of the "losers" of faith. The longing is not unique to that historical group; it is the cultural ethos of maternal societies in general to desire motherly-relatedness with others, including gods.[9] While in a patriarchal society the father has the authority and power (superego, to use the Freudian language) to regulate the conduct of the child (id) with clear rules and punish-ment (fear of castration), in a maternal society it is the mother's love of the erring child that brings about a reconciliation. In the latter, vio-lence or confrontation is avoided, and peace and harmony are optimis-

---

6. Shusako Endo, Hideo Uefusa, et al., *Bosei To Seisei* ["Motherliness and holiness"] (Tokyo: Kyobunkwan, 1973), p. 170.

7. Shusako Endo, *A Life of Jesus*, trans. Richard A. Schuchert (New York: Paulist, 1978); Endo, *Kirisuto No Tanjo* ["The birth of Christ"] (Tokyo: Shincho, 1982).

8. Shusako Endo, "Ihojin No Kuno" ["Agony of Gentiles"], in *Endo Shusaku Bungaku Zenshu* ["All works of Shusaku Endo"] (Tokyo: Shincho, 2000), vol. 13. Endo confesses in this essay that by writing *Silence* (with its emphasis on the motherly aspects of the Chris-tian God) he felt that the gap between Christianity and himself was somewhat filled.

9. For Japan as a maternal society, see Tomiko Yoda, "The Rise and Fall of Mater-nal Society: Gender, Labor, and Capital in Contemporary Japan," *South Atlantic Quar-terly* 99, no. 4 (Fall 2000): 860-902.

tically (or naïvely) expected within a society. Such a society, however, does not necessarily emphasize the importance of establishing one's individual selfhood. Thus, "my children are all good children" in the maternal society, while "only good children are my children" in the patriarchal society.[10] Longing for such relatedness is reflected, for example, in the genesis mythology of the Japanese imperial history in *Kojiki* (Record of Ancient Things, compiled in 712 C.E.), in which the female sun god, Amaterasu, is peacefully enthroned as the supreme god and relates with other deities as a mother in a sort of indulging way,[11] unlike a typical kingdom myth in which a male god becomes a supreme being by winning the final victory after fierce battles.[12]

Is the maternal longing for God, then, to be regarded as a form of syncretism, as Ferreira of *Silence* condemns the Japanese faith in Christ as "not our God"? Such a judgment seems to depend too much on a patriarchal worldview. With only this view at hand, one may not be able to appreciate fully the riches of who God is. Though the longing for motherliness might be somewhat inflated in the maternal society,[13] that excessive sensitivity may help to point out possible neglected aspects of God in the traditional theological discussion. Indeed, a review of theological textbooks reveals that the parental image of God's relatedness to humans is focused solely on the designation of God as "Father."[14] It seems, then, appropriate to be attentive to the evaluation

10. Hayao Kawai and Osamu Fujita, *Do Kangaeru Ka — Haha Naru Mono* ["How do we think of motherliness?"] (Tokyo: Nigensha, 1977), pp. 164-68. K. Tsuruta, a literary critic, says that while Western novels generally depict the growth of the main character, such a bildungsroman is rare in Japanese novels. Rather, a Japanese hero or heroine often goes on a journey to regress or return to the mother's womb on the way. Kinya Tsuruta, *Haha Naru Mono To Sei Naru Mono* [*Motherliness and Holiness*] (Tokyo: Meiji Shoin, 1986), pp. 3-4.

11. See O-no-Yasumaro, *Kojiki* ["Record of ancient things"], trans. Donald L. Philippi (Tokyo: University of Tokyo Press, 1968).

12. For example, Zeus against Cronus and Titan in the Greek mythology, and Marduk against Tiamat in the Babylonian mythology.

13. Takeo Doi explains that the Japanese way of relatedness with others may reflect the pathological overdependence on their parents, in this case especially on their mothers. Doi, *The Anatomy of Dependence*, trans. John Bester (Tokyo: Kodansha, 1973).

14. Ladd focuses solely on the fatherly relatedness of God in the discussion of Theology proper in the Synoptic Gospels. George E. Ladd, *A Theology of the New Testament*, rev. ed. (Grand Rapids: Eerdmans, 1993), pp. 82-85. Erickson refers to the parental metaphor of father in his discussion of the trinitarian confession. Millard J. Erickson, *Christian Theology* (Grand Rapids: Baker, 1983). The one-sided description of the parental metaphor

of feminist exegetes in Western societies that motherly aspects are largely neglected in the traditional discussion of God.[15] Indeed, the renowned feminist author Ursula Le Guin proposes that the language that embodies motherly relatedness ("mother tongue") be given rightful place alongside "father tongue" in order to attain the sound human communicative experience ("native tongue").[16] The present cultural reading overlaps greatly with the feminist reading, while the latter is primarily concerned with gender and the former with relatedness.

It is not the intention of this chapter to merely add some presumably positive feminine features to the masculine deity in order to make "him" appear a tenderer and warmer father. Elizabeth Johnson, a prominent feminist theologian, criticizes some gender-sensitive readings of Scripture that attempt to discover feminine traits of God in the biblical texts but only result in affirming traditional androcentric theology.[17]

---

for God is never questioned, but rather assumed. Leon Morris, *New Testament Theology* (Grand Rapids: Zondervan, 1986), pp. 248-55. Gaventa points out that the traditional systematic theological discussion largely neglects the implication in Paul's gospel for the lives of women. She takes the example of James D. G. Dunn's New Testament theology. Beverly R. Gaventa, "Is Galatians Just A 'Guy Thing'? A Theological Reflection," *Interpretation* 54 (2000): 267-78 (269). See James D. G. Dunn, *The Theology of Paul the Apostle* (Grand Rapids: Eerdmans, 1998). While the yearning of motherliness may be more evident in maternal societies, it is to some degree universally felt. It has been suggested by such prominent psychoanalysts as Freud and Jung that humans develop their self-understanding and relatedness to others at least partly in the relation to their mothers. Sigmund Freud, *On Sexuality: Three Essays on the Theory of Sexuality and Other Works*, trans. James Strachey (London: Penguin, 1991); Carl G. Jung, *Four Archetypes: Mother, Rebirth, Spirit, Trickster* (London: Ark, 1972). Kawai, a Jungian psychoanalyst, explains that the presence of Great Mother is so strong in maternal societies that it is almost impossible for a child to confront the swallowing mother, let alone to kill her. H. Kawai, *Muishiki No Kozo* ["Structure of unconsciousness"] (Tokyo: Chuko Shinsho, 1977), pp. 90-91.

15. Phyllis Trible, "Feminist Hermeneutics and Biblical Studies," *Christian Century* (1982): 116.

16. Ursula Le Guin, *Dancing at the Edge of the World: Thoughts on Words, Women, Places* (New York: Grove, 1989), pp. 147-60. The power of mother tongue in comparison with father tongue, according to Le Guin, "is not in dividing but in binding, not in distancing but in uniting" (p. 149). Eastman uses Le Guin's concept to interpret Paul in Galatians. Suzan Eastman, *Recovering Paul's Mother Tongue* (Grand Rapids: Eerdmans, 2007).

17. Elizabeth A. Johnson, *She Who Is: The Mystery of God in Feminist Theological Discourse* (New York: Crossroad, 1992), pp. 48-49. She comments on such an attempt, saying, "Men gain their feminine side, but women do not gain their masculine side. The feminine is there for the enhancement of the male, but not vice-versa: there is no mutual gain."

The present search for motherliness is rather to show that the biblical writers are aware that both paternal metaphors and maternal metaphors (including the very designations of "father" and "mother") are requisite in directing the reader into the mystery of God. One should be aware that the biblical metaphors are significant but only partial and finite tools for describing and explaining the divine reality.[18] Therefore, God is like a father, but never equal to my biological father. One should note that the church decided to employ metaphors to compose the creedal confession, "We believe in God the Father . . ."[19] When Johnson suggests the feminist Trinity of Spirit-Sophia, Jesus-Sophia, and Mother-Sophia, she uses terms that are also metaphors. Each metaphor is partial and finite, never perfect and full. Only when proper metaphors are employed together may we come closer to experiencing the divine mystery.[20]

This essay may be able to contribute to our discussion of God by focusing on how God relates to humans in Scripture. *Motherliness* (as well as fatherliness), being an emotionally loaded word, is rather difficult to define. Some characteristic relational features of maternity are suggested in relation to those of paternity by psychoanalysts and comparative mythologists; for example: inclusion in relation to exclusion, embrace to separation, nourishment to discipline, sympathy to condemnation, and forgiveness to punishment.[21] These antitheses will be kept in mind as the analysis of the text is conducted in the following section. Incidentally, such binary descriptions in the feminist discussion — usually focusing on the character differences between femininity and masculinity — are sometimes considered to reflect a homosocial value judgment.[22] Sarah Coakley's point, therefore, seems appropriate when she surveys a vari-

---

18. Paul Tillich, *Dynamics of Faith* (New York: Harper & Row, 1957), pp. 41-48. Cf. Paul Ricoeur, *The Rule of Metaphor: The Creation of Meaning in Language*, trans. R. Czerny, K. McLaughlin, and J. Costello (London: Routledge, 2003).

19. See Sallie McFague, *Metaphorical Theology: Models of God in Religious Language* (Philadelphia: Fortress, 1982), pp. 103-44. She comments, "Credal language is both deceptive and powerful; hence, the temptations to idolatry are strong. It is deceptive because it looks like literal language" (p. 115). See also McFague, *Speaking in Parables: A Study in Metaphor and Theology* (Philadelphia: Fortress, 1975), pp. 43-65.

20. McFague, *Metaphorical Theology*, pp. 115, 177.

21. Kawai, *Muishiki no Kozo*; Atsuhiko Yoshida, *Nihon Shinwa No Shinso Shinri* ["Depth psychology of Japanese mythology"] (Tokyo: Yamato Shobo, 2012).

22. Rosemary R. Ruether, *Sexism and God-Talk: Towards A Feminist Theology* (London: SCM, 1983), p. 111.

ety of Enlightenment thinkers and criticizes their dualistic view of "domestic and irrational female vs. social and rational male," which affirmed a traditional patriarchal social construct in which women, playing a submissive role under the authority of men, were deprived of equal human rights.[23]

Two points should be briefly noted. First, one wonders whether such ideas as inclusion, embrace, nourishment, sympathy, and forgiveness must necessarily be associated with domesticity, irrationality, and therefore submission. The former ideas may be liberated from such politically intentional languages as the latter, when one takes into consideration the aforementioned Amaterasu, the supreme goddess in *Kojiki*, who reigns over all gods and humans, yet as a mother is ready to include, embrace, nourish, sympathize, and forgive.[24] Second, when one exegetes a text, she or he should be aware that its meanings are conveyed through culturally and historically conditioned words. One's task is primarily not to make an ethical judgment of the culture in history, though it could well be done later. When the Scripture uses the metaphor of "father" and "birthing" to describe God, one must first of all ask what picture of God is conveyed with the paternal and maternal metaphors in the historical culture. Then the discussion as to whether those metaphors are appropriate for postmodern sensibilities can be meaningfully begun and maintained.[25] The present chapter is located well within the former process, but not in negligence of the latter discussion.

The present analysis focuses on Paul's Letter to the Galatians. The reason for focusing on this text is that it is one of the earliest writings of the church and therefore naturally reflects its earliest understanding of God. Another reason is that Paul is popularly criticized as

23. Sarah Coakley, *Powers and Submissions: Spirituality, Philosophy and Gender*, Challenges in Contemporary Theology (Oxford: Blackwell, 2002), pp. 89-97.

24. Ruether's criticism of liberal feminism is, therefore, appreciated. However, her argument for women's rather than men's capacity for greater integration as a human seems to be somewhat doubtful and above all unnecessary in the nature and course of the discussion. Ruether, *Sexism and God-Talk*, pp. 109-15.

25. Should we replace parental metaphors altogether with the metaphor of friendship? See the discussion in McFague, *Metaphorical Theology*, pp. 184-92. Parental metaphors have much to do with the family metaphor for the Christian community. Questioning the former metaphors may reduce the value of the latter metaphor. Should the value of the traditional institution of marriage be reevaluated?

a "chauvinist" theologian who may consequently be expected to en-
courage a paternal understanding of God.[26] If, then, maternal aspects
are found even in Paul's theology, maternal theology may be found not
altogether foreign to the earliest thinkers and writers of the church.

II. Motherliness of God in Galatians

"Male and Female" as the Image of God (Gal. 3:28)

**A. The Structure of Galatians 3–4 and the Significance of the Baptis-
mal Triple Couplets** It is generally understood that chapters 3 and 4 of
Galatians form the theoretical core of the entire letter.[27] In this section
of the letter, Paul repeatedly asks who the true heirs of Abraham are.
In the traditional Jewish perspective, Paul's opponents contend that
the true Abrahamic heirs are those circumcised under the Law. The
masculine initiatory rite of circumcision affirms the hierarchical institution based on the paternal genealogy – fathers begetting sons – in
which people are ranked and excluded on account of various material
differences. In refuting this patriarchal relatedness, Paul emphasizes
faith in Christ as the one and only determining factor for inclusion
in the Abrahamic family. If paternal relatedness is thus regulated in
Galatians 3, it is understandable that the maternal language suddenly
becomes conspicuous in Galatians 4 in order for Paul to keep the balance in his theological discussion.[28] Therefore, one encounters in the

---

26. See J. R. Daniel Kirk, *Jesus Have I Loved, but Paul? A Narrative Approach to the Problem of Pauline Christianity* (Grand Rapids: Baker Academic, 2011), p. 5. See also Gaventa,
who attempts to read something more in Paul's Letter to the Galatians, which seems
to be a "guy thing." She shares her experience that "for many seminarians, pastors,
and laypeople with whom I have talked, it is simply assumed that women will read
Paul with suspicion, even with hostility." See Gaventa, "Is Pauline Theology Just a
'Guy Thing'?" chap. 5 in *Our Mother Saint Paul* (Louisville: Westminster John Knox,
2007), pp. 63-75 (here p. 65).

27. Hans D. Betz, *Galatians*, Hermeneia (Philadelphia: Fortress, 1979), p. 128;
F. F. Bruce, *The Epistle to the Galatians*, NIGTC (Grand Rapids: Eerdmans, 1982), p. 214;
James D. G. Dunn, *The Epistle to the Galatians*, BNTC (Peabody, Mass.: Hendrickson,
1993), p. 243.

28. Brigitte Kahl, "No Longer Male: Masculinity Struggles behind Galatians 3:28?,"
JSNT 79 (2000): 41-43. In Kahl's expressions, Galatians 3 is "decentering the male" and
Galatians 4 is "recentering the female." It may be that in the expression "male and

fourth chapter Jesus' mother (v. 4), the story of Sarah and Hagar as mothers (vv. 21-31), and Paul as a mother in birth pain (v. 19).[29] Thus paternal relatedness of differentiation and exclusion is counterbalanced by maternal relatedness of unification and inclusion.[30]

In the climax of Paul's presentation of anti-phallocratic salvation history stands the emancipatory announcement: "There is no longer Jew or Greek, there is no longer slave or free, there is no longer male and female" (Gal. 3:28). With the background of the ethnic identity issue in Galatians 2 – whether one needs to be a Jew to belong to the church – the first ethnic couplet of "Jew or Greek" is usually considered to be Paul's primary concern among the three couplets.[31] However, if Paul's salvation history is viewed as a critique of the excessive emphasis on the paternal relatedness that privileges Jewish male masters over against others, then the erasure of difference in all of the three couplets should be regarded as significant: Paul realizes the fullness of humanity and riches of relatedness among such humans in the community in Christ. Therefore, in this triple-couplet baptismal formula Paul is envisioning the communal experience of original humanity – "in Christ you are all children of God through faith" (3:26) – especially for the marginalized members of the community.[32] While the eradication of all three levels of difference is equally important in the community, Paul may have seen the couplet of "male and female" as outstanding because it directly points to the original state of humanity.

B. "Male and Female" and the Understanding of God The third couplet, "male and female," clearly declares the eradication of gender dif-

---

female" in Gal. 3:28 Paul is envisioning some sort of convergence of paternity and maternity.

29. Kahl calls Galatians 4 the "mother-chapter" of Paul. Kahl, "No Longer Male," p. 43.

30. In the language of liminal theology, the former relatedness is "anti-liminal (= institutional and hierarchical)" while the latter relatedness is "liminal (= anti-institutional and egalitarian)." See Victor Turner, *The Ritual Process: Structure and Anti-Structure* (New York: Cornell University Press, 1969); Christian Strecker, *Die liminale Theologie des Paulus: Zugänge zu paulinischen Theologie aus kulturanthropologischen Perspektive*, FRLANT 185 (Göttingen: Vandenhoeck & Ruprecht, 1999).

31. See Richard N. Longenecker, *Galatians*, WBC 41 (Dallas: Word, 1990), pp. 156-57.

32. Atsuhiro Asano, *Community-Identity Construction in Galatians: Exegetical, Social-Anthropological and Socio-Historical Studies*, JSNTSup 285 (London: T&T Clark, 2005), pp. 187-206.

ference. In Christ, there is no difference between male members and female members of the community; "for all of you are one [person] in Christ Jesus" (Gal. 3:28). Behind such a relatedness lies a view of God reflected in the creation story.

Exegetes have suggested that Paul had in mind the creation narrative of Genesis as he penned the third couplet.[33] While the other couplets use the connective "nor," the third couplet uses "and": "male *and* female [*arsen kai thēly*]," not "male *nor* female." It has been argued that Paul uses the irregular "and" as in "male and female" because he draws the expression directly from LXX Gen. 1:27, which says, "and God created humankind [*ton anthrōpon*], according to the image of God he created him, *male and female* [*arsen kai thēly*] he created them." In the Second Temple and rabbinic periods, the fact that Genesis has two accounts of the creation of humankind invited the speculation that original humanity ("heavenly man" in Genesis 1) is androgynous, "male and female" at the same time (Philo, *Leg. all.* 1.31-32; *Megilla* 9a; *Gen. Rab.* 8.1, 17.6). Probably influenced by the androgynous union in the passage rite of the Greco-Oriental religions, Philo thought that the "earthly man" (Genesis 2) will be transformed and return to the androgynous image of God (*Quaest. in Gen.* 1.25; cf. *Vit. cont.* 63).[34] Even though Paul himself may not have taught that the image of God was androgynous, his audience was most probably aware of such a worldview in their Greco-Oriental background.[35] Then, "male and female" as the original humanity in the image of God may have been a quite helpful locution to express the vision of the perfect union and equality among the Pauline churches.

The book of Genesis, after narrating the actual creation of the universe, discloses the divine identity as early as in Gen. 1:27. In the Hebrew Bible more than in the LXX, the chiasmic construction empha-

---

33. There is a possibility that Paul is quoting a baptismal saying formed before him among the early believers. Elisabeth Schüssler Fiorenza, *In Memory of Her: A Feminist Theological Reconstruction of Christian Origins* (London: SCM, 1983), p. 209. However, it is possible that it was formulated by Paul and taught among the believers in his first visit to Galatia.

34. See Wayne A. Meeks, "The Image of the Androgyne: Some Uses of a Symbol in Earliest Christianity," *History of Religions* 13 (1973-1974): 165-208.

35. Dennis R. MacDonald, *There Is No Male and Female: The Fate of a Dominical Saying in Paul and Gnosticism* (Philadelphia: Fortress, 1987), p. 63. Schüssler Fiorenza understands that "male and female" implies the patriarchal marriage system and that Paul is saying that such a system is no longer constitutive in the new community. *In Memory of Her*, p. 211.

sizes that the divine image is revealed in the creation of humankind. It is significant that at the very beginning of Scripture the image of God is revealed in terms of male and female. In the phrase "God created humankind in his image," the object of creation is "the Adam [*h'dm*]" *(ton anthrōpon)*. The articular noun – Adam with a definite article – suggests that it is not an individual Adam but humankind in general.[36] God's creation of humankind in its "wholeness" of male and female reflects the image of the Creator. In other words, both the masculine imagery and the feminine imagery need to be employed in the expression of God in order for humans to begin embracing a sound view of God. Since God is the creative source of humankind, as well as the rest of creation, metaphors of both father and mother can be properly applied to the deity. A lack of awareness of the maternal imagery along with excessive emphasis on the paternal imagery fails to present the fuller picture of who he is. In establishing his community and presenting the new salvation history, for example in Paul's ecclesiology and soteriology, a more holistic view of God is reflected.

C. **Motherliness in the God of Israel** The theology behind Paul's vision of a full and rich union of believers in his community prompts him to describe God with maternal imagery found in the Hebrew Bible. Therefore, "womb [*rḥm*]" is often the physical locus in which God's will is revealed (Sarah in Gen. 20:1-18; Leah in Gen. 29:31-35; Hannah in 1 Sam. 1:1-20). The same Hebrew radicals *(rḥm)* in plural form denotes "mercy" or "compassion." Rachel's mourning over the lost fruit of her womb (Ephraim) is met by God's mercy through the child in the divine womb (Jer. 31:15-23).[37] "Therefore, my inner parts / womb [*m'h*] trembles for him, I will truly show motherly compassion [*rḥm*] upon him" (v. 20). God's merciful dealing and saving grace is very closely related to the image of a mother giving birth to a child and breastfeeding the child (Ps. 22:9-10; Isa. 46:3-4). Divine mercy is expressed in motherly terms. God indeed says that "I will cry out like a woman in labor, I will gasp and pant" (Isa. 42:14). When Trible claims that "relinquishing life for the sake of life is the last act of the uterus,"[38] the quintessential ma-

36. Gordon J. Wenham, *Genesis 1–15*, WBC 1 (Dallas: Word, 1987), pp. 32-33.

37. Phyllis Trible, *God and the Rhetoric of Sexuality*, Overtures to Biblical Theology (Philadelphia: Fortress, 1979), p. 45.

38. Trible, *God and the Rhetoric of Sexuality*, p. 37.

ternal act almost forecasts the act of Christ on the cross to embrace the sinful children and to writhe for them by bearing upon himself their sins. Then what one finds on the face of Christ is not, or at least not only, the paternity of God that defines and concretizes sin on the cross for condemnation,[39] but the maternal body of God that internalizes the sin of humanity and groans with it.[40] Indeed, in 2 Cor. 5:21, where Paul says, "he made him to be sin who knew no sin," attention tends to be directed to the paternity defining sin, yet in the act of imbuement of sin the maternity embracing sin may well be implied.[41] Probably the most direct and impressive connection of God and mother is found in Deut. 32:18, "You were unmindful of the Rock that begot you, and you forgot the God who writhed in childbirth." Paul may have had this image in mind when he reminded the Galatians how he was relating to them.

Imitation of the Writhing God (Gal. 4:19)

A. Paul's Motherly Labor At the conclusion of probably the most emotional section of the letter (Gal. 4:12-20) comes a surprising expression of Paul's relatedness to the Galatians: "My little children, for whom I am writhing again in childbirth [*ōdinō*] until Christ is formed in you" (4:19). The appearance of the maternal expression is startling in two ways.[42] First, the imagery concerning children and maturity in the early part of the chapter (4:1-3) is now chronologically upset by the imagery of the pain of childbirth that naturally foregoes maturity.[43] Second and more importantly, Paul elsewhere explicitly describes his role in relation to his community members as a "father," in the sense

39. Keigo Okonogi, *Nihon-Jin no Ajase Konpurekusu* ("Japanese Ajase Complex") (Tokyo: Chuo Koron, 1982), p. 30.

40. Endo, "Kami No Chinmoku To Ningen No Shogen."

41. Paul, in this verse, may primarily have had the picture of a scapegoat taking on the sin (curse) of the people of Israel in the expulsion rite (Lev. 16:20-22; see Gal. 3:13). The passive acceptance of the scapegoat (or *pharmakos* in the corresponding Hellenistic rites) may be a helpful metaphor to remind us of the maternity of God.

42. Commentators generally find the expression to be surprising in the letter as well as in the rest of Paul's Letters. Ernest De Witt Burton, *The Epistle to the Galatians*, ICC (Edinburgh: T&T Clark, 1921), p. 248; J. Louis Martyn, *Galatians*, ABC 33A (New York: Doubleday, 1997), p. 424.

43. Dunn, *Galatians*, p. 240.

of spiritually begetting believers in Christ in his mission and developing them. Therefore, "in Christ Jesus I became your father through the
gospel" (1 Cor. 4:15), and "we deal with each one of you like a father
with his children" (1 Thess. 2:11; see also Phlm. 10). We should note,
however, that in 1 Thessalonians Paul balances his role as a father with
that of a mother, so in the immediately preceding section he says, "we
were gentle among you, like a [nursing] mother [*trophos*] tenderly caring for her own children" (2:7).[44]

A maternal self-designation by Paul is not, therefore, absent in the
rest of the Pauline Letters. However, his use of the word *ōdinō*, and the
vivid image of motherhood it implies, is impressive. Paul elsewhere
uses the word only twice for the cosmic turbulence in the eschatological context (Rom. 8:22; 1 Thess. 5:3). The extraordinary word choice —
reflecting something physically impossible for Paul — is highly intentional and possibly conditions the reader to read the whole pericope
as if it were written by their mother. Though the pericope is often
thought of as "an interruption" in the flow of argument in Galatians
3–4,[45] it could be explained as Paul's creative rhetoric to appeal to the
pathos of the readers.[46]

Ōdinō means "to experience pain and anguish through childbirth,"
and the noun form *ōdin* means "birthpang" (Isa. 23:4; 26:17-18; 45:10;
51:2; 54:1; 66:7-8; Jer. 4:31; 30:6; Mic. 4:10). "Behold, she suffered birth
pain [*ōdinēsen*] for unrighteousness, she seized pain and gave birth [*ete-
ken*] to lawlessness" (Ps. 7:14). Here, the psalmist uses two verbs (*ōdinō*
and *tiktō*) to describe childbirth, but the former especially focuses on
the suffering of a mother in the action of childbirth. Therefore, the

---

44. The word *trophos* is elsewhere translated as "nurse" (see NRSV or Malherbe).
Abraham J. Malherbe, *The Letters to the Thessalonians*, ABC 32B (New York: Doubleday,
2000), p. 146. Or "wet nurse," in Gene L. Green, *The Letters to the Thessalonians*, PNTC
(Grand Rapids: Eerdmans, 2002). However, it could well be "nursing mother" or even
"mother." Charles A. Wanamaker, *The Epistles to the Thessalonians*, NIGTC (Grand Rapids:
Eerdmans, 1990), p. 100. See also Walter Bauer et al., *A Greek-English Lexicon of the New
Testament and Other Early Christian Literature*, 2nd ed. (Chicago: University of Chicago
Press, 1979), pp. 827-28.

45. Burton, *Galatians*, p. 235; Franz Mußner, *Der Galaterbrief*, HTKNT 9 (Freiburg:
Herder, 1981), p. 304.

46. Eastman sees the larger pericope of Gal. 4:12–5:1 as written in the "mother
tongue" to make the bridge between the preceding theoretical section and the following paraenetic section. Eastman, *Recovering Paul's Mother Tongue*. Cf. Burton, *Galatians*,
p. 236.

suffering of the day of the Lord before the messianic age is described by the metaphor of *ōdinō/ōdin* (1 *En.* 62.4; 4 *Esdr.* 4.42). In the Gospels, as well as the Pauline texts referred to above, the term is used in the context of apocalyptic suffering before the new heaven and earth are given birth. "There will be earthquakes in various places; there will be famines. These are the beginning of the birth pangs [*ōdinōn*]" (Mark 13:8; cf. Matt. 24:8). The end-time suffering, intensified by the metaphor of birth pain, enhances by comparison the salvific jubilance that follows.[47] Therefore, Gaventa understands Paul's use of *ōdinō* in Gal. 4:19 in the apocalyptic sense, that is, Paul's missionary "labor" among the Galatians points to the suffering of this age awaiting the fulfillment of salvation in Christ.[48] Considering that Galatians is probably the most apocalyptic of Paul's letters (given the revelation of God's Son in Paul [1:15-16] and among the Galatians [3:1-5]), the present pericope and especially 4:19 could well be considered to reflect Paul's eschatology. If Paul's mimesis of the suffering Christ — Paul suffers as Christ suffers for salvation — is expressed in the apocalyptic language of *ōdinō*, the relationship of his Christology and his eschatology — Christ suffers as the earth suffers before the joy of salvation — may be glimpsed in this verse. Furthermore, behind these thoughts may lie the view of a God who suffers for his people.[49]

Isaiah 45:10 describes God as a mother suffering pain in giving birth to his people Israel: "The one saying to the father 'what will you give birth to?' or to the mother 'what will you suffer birth pain [*ōdinēseis*] for?'" Here, the creation of Israel is in focus as there were people who doubted their divine origin. Martyn finds this verse in Isaiah to be behind Paul's expression in Gal. 4:19.[50] However, probably closer to the context of Paul's missionary suffering is the Song of Moses in Deut. 32:1-43, in which God is described as writhing in birth pain (v. 18) for wayward Israel. Curiously the LXX translates this verse rather freely, though retaining the maternal features of God. "You forsook God giving birth to you, and forgot God feeding [*trephontos*] you." Yet the MT

47. Georg Bertram, "*ōdin/ōdinō*," in *Theological Dictionary of the New Testament*, ed. Gerhard Kittel and Gerhard Friedrich, trans. Geoffrey W. Bromiley (Grand Rapids: Eerdmans, 1974), 9:672-74.

48. Gaventa, *Our Mother*, pp. 32-34.

49. Both Martyn and Eastman find in *ōdinō* of Gal. 4:19 the pain of God. Martyn, *Galatians*, pp. 428-29; Eastman, *Mother Tongue*, pp. 120-21.

50. Martyn, *Galatians*, p. 429.

has it as "You were unmindful of the Rock that begot you [*yld*], and you forgot the God who writhed in childbirth [*ḥûl*]." *Ḥûl* means "to writhe" especially in the pain of childbirth (Isa. 26:17; 45:10);[51] therefore, the Greek term *ōdinō* is the natural translation of the Hebrew word as in Isa. 45:10. In the Song of Moses, which gives the history of a wayward Israel, God's tender care is sadly not met by the faithful response of his children. Through the grief-laden experience of child-rearing, Israel is reminded of their father creating them (Deut. 32:6) and of their mother birthing them (Deut. 32:18). They should not ignore the authority of fatherly creation nor disregard the pain of motherly procreation.[52] Therefore, Paul's bewilderment and perplexity over the waywardness of the Galatians with respect to the messages of Paul and of his opponents in the pericope (Gal. 4:12-20) seem to mirror the motherly anguish of God in drawing unfaithful Israel ever nearer to his/her bosom. God as a mother suffers birth pain for Israel; therefore, Paul imitates God in suffering birth pain for the Galatians as their mother. Thus Paul's missionary relatedness as seen in this pericope reflects his view of a God who relates to his people as a mother does to her children.[53]

B. Motherly Motivation of the Salvific Pattern At the beginning of the pericope (Gal. 4:12), Paul entreats the Galatians by presenting a curious pattern of unity. "Become as I am, for I also have become as you are." Considering the exigency of the letter, Paul is most probably urging the Galatians to be like Paul, who stands outside the law for the truth of the gospel, as Paul became like the Galatian Gentiles without the law for the truth of the gospel.[54] Paul elsewhere says, "To those outside the law I became as one outside the law" (1 Cor. 9:21). Such a stance to the law probably invited some form of persecution by parts of law-observant Jews, which is a cause for Paul's missionary suffering (2 Cor. 11:16-33). In the unity of Paul and the Galatians, salvation is to

---

51. Francis Brown et al., eds., *The New Brown-Driver-Briggs-Gesenius Hebrew and English Lexicon* (Peabody, Mass.: Hendrickson, 1979), pp. 296-97; Laird Harris et al., eds., *Theological Wordbook of the Old Testament* (Chicago: Moody Press, 1980), 1:270-71.

52. Therefore, *yld* and *ḥûl* represent the act of a mother, instead of *yld* pointing to a father's act and *ḥûl* pointing to a mother's act. For *yld* as denoting the birth of a mother, see Prov. 23:22. Trible, *God and the Rhetoric of Sexuality*, pp. 62-63.

53. Being well aware of the Masoretic presentation of God, Paul's image may be closer to the context of Deut. 32:18 than Isa. 45:10.

54. Burton, *Galatians*, pp. 236-37; Dunn, *Galatians*, pp. 232-33.

be reached. In the salvific pattern, Paul suffers and the suffering brings the Galatians closer to Paul. Paul describes the goal of this salvation process as "Christ is formed in you" (Gal. 4:19). Therefore, the reader is naturally reminded of the christological motivation of Paul's missionary suffering.[55] Indeed, the immediately preceding pericope presents the salvific pattern in the history of God's Son. The Son of God was "born of a woman, born under the law . . . so that we might receive adoption as children" (4:4-5). In other words, the Son of God became like us, so we become the children of God. In a more developed form of salvific pattern, "[God] made him to be sin who knew no sin, so that in him we might become the righteousness of God" (2 Cor. 5:21). In the unity of God's Son and humanity, salvation is to be reached. In the salvific pattern, God's Son suffers the vulnerability of humanity, and that suffering brings humans closer to the Son. Furthermore, Christ's salvific passion reflects how God as a mother suffers for Israel.[56] In the history of Israel, God as a mother embraced the vulnerability of his/her children Israel, thus becoming vulnerable her/himself in the pregnancy, and Israel is nurtured to reflect her image. In the unity of God and Israel, salvation is to be reached. In the salvific pattern, God as a mother suffers the vulnerability of Israel, and the suffering brings Israel closer to God. If such a motherly relatedness and unity is the motivation of Paul's dealing with the Galatians, the deconstructionist criticism that Paul's mimesis command — "become like me" — reveals his patriarchal authoritarianism[57] should indeed be reconsidered.[58]

If God's salvation of humanity is described in terms of motherly relatedness to her children, it is understandable that Paul in Galatians refers to the maternal origin of the salvific acts. Thus, for the revelation of God's Son and the call to the Gentile mission, Paul was divinely ordained in his mother's womb (Gal. 1:15-16). In the decisive moment of salvation history, Jesus was born of a woman (4:4). The gospel of

55. Eastman, *Mother Tongue*, pp. 64-65.

56. Eastman argues that as prophets embodied God's suffering for his people, Paul in his persecution enacts the suffering of Christ. Eastman, "Paul among the Prophets" (pp. 63-88), in *Mother Tongue*, esp. pp. 72-73. I tend to see that God's suffering is reflected in Christ's suffering, and in turn it is reflected in Paul's suffering.

57. Elizabeth A. Castelli, *Imitating Paul: A Discourse of Power* (Louisville: Westminster John Knox, 1991), pp. 86-87; Elisabeth Schüssler Fiorenza, *Rhetoric and Ethic: Politics of Biblical Studies* (Minneapolis: Fortress, 1999), pp. 164-65.

58. Kahl, "No Longer Male," pp. 45-46; Eastman, *Mother Tongue*, p. 86.

Christ is to bear fruit among the Galatians because of Paul's birth pangs (4:19). Furthermore, the eschatological community, Jerusalem above, is "our mother," in whom regeneration is experienced (4:26-27).

III. Epilogue: Toward a Holistic View of God

Behind Paul's vision of the perfect union in his community lies a view of God whose image is the perfect union of "male and female." It is therefore natural that God is presented metaphorically as both a father and a mother in Scripture. Without appreciating the maternal aspect of God, one may lose sight of the divine intention for God's church. When Paul related to the Galatians as a missionary-pastor, he imitated a God who, as a mother in agony, internalized the vulnerability of Israel. Paul may well have been aware that the maternal relatedness and unity of God was a chief motivation energizing the salvific activities of humanity. Without appreciating the maternal inspiration of the God of the salvific mission, one may misunderstand the divine intention as to how humanity is to be touched by God. Therefore, the theology that fully recognizes the motherliness of God, which painfully embraces vulnerable others, may nurture followers of Christ to reach the richness of Christian being. Yet in the history of the church, commentators and translators have at times been quite conditioned by the paternal worldview. John Chrysostom, for example, comments on the birth pain of Paul in Gal. 4:19; "Did you see his *paternal* care [*splanchna patrika*]? Did you see the anxiety of the apostle's worth? Did you see how he sent out cries much more fierce than of those in labor?"[59] And more recently, the Jerusalem Bible translates Deut. 32:18b as "unmindful now of the God who *fathered* you."

In the early church some attempts were made to preserve a maternal sensitivity toward God, though efforts to secure "orthodoxy" tended to sacrifice this sensitivity. For example, among the second-century Syriac churches, God was portrayed as having two breasts full of milk and giving milk to the world out of his (her) breasts, with the Holy Spirit milking him (*Odes of Solomon* 19.1-4). Probably this maternal expression of God influenced the Syriac translation of John 1:18;

---

59. John Chrysostom, *"Hypomnēma eis tēn pros Galatas epistolēn,"* in *Patrologiae Cursus Completus, Series Graeca,* ed. Jacques Paul Migne (Paris: Gaume Fratres, 1857-66), 61.2:660.

whereas in Greek "the only Son . . . is close to the Father's bosom [*kolpon,*]" in Syriac he is close to God's womb *('ubba).* The interest in the maternal aspects of God among the Syriac churches seemed to be gradually directed toward or limited to the description of the Holy Spirit. Therefore in the *Acts of Thomas,* the Holy Spirit is a "compassionate mother" (2:27) and "hidden mother" (5:50). This theological tendency is probably preserved in the *Gospel of Philip,* which points out the error of viewing Mary as conceiving by the Holy Spirit, asking, "When did a woman ever conceive by a woman?" (17a). That is, "the power of the Most High [= the word]," rather than the female Spirit, is responsible for Mary's giving birth to Jesus (see Luke 1:35).[60] Aphrahat, "the Persian Sage," who lived during the fourth-century Sassanid dynasty, reflects this old Syrian pneumatology in his expression "Father God and Mother Spirit" *(Demonstrations* 18).[61] Alongside this maternal understanding of the Godhead an androgynous speculation of the Trinity among the Gnostics was developed. The *Apocryphon of John* seems to assume a trinity of *propatēr* ("original father"), *pronoia* ("foreknowledge"), and *autogenēs* ("one coming to being"). *Pronoia* confesses to be both father and mother *(metropatēr),* and it is also called the spirit (see 2-5). Probably because of the possible association with Gnostic theology, the Syriac churches started in the fifth century to move away from viewing the Holy Spirit as feminine.[62] The Syriac translation for the Greek *pneuma* (the neuter word for "spirit") is *ruḥa,* and it is feminine, as is the Hebrew *rûaḥ.* Therefore in the Old Syriac version (a translation of the late second to third century), the Holy Spirit is consistently treated as feminine grammatically. Yet in the Peshitta of the fifth century, the Holy Spirit began to be treated as masculine, and in the Harklean version of the early seventh century, it became masculine throughout. The longing for motherliness in the Christian religion is then directed

---

60. S. P. Brock, "Passover, Annunciation and Epiclesis: Some Remarks on the Term *Aggen* in the Syriac Version of Luke 1:35," *Novum Testamentum* 24 (1984): 227. On the discussion of maternal pneumatology among the Syriac churches, see Fumihiko Takeda, "Josei to shite no Seirei" ["The Holy Spirit as feminine in the early Syriac Christian tradition"], *Theological Studies in Japan* 47 (2008): 59-86.

61. On motherliness of the Syriac theology, see Robert Murray, *Symbols of Church and Kingdom: A Study in Early Syriac Tradition* (Cambridge: Cambridge University Press, 1975), pp. 131-58.

62. Takeda, "Josei to shite no Seirei," p. 70.

to and contained in the reverence of Mary, the mother of Jesus.[63] Despite the opposition of Nestorius in the christological discussion, Mary was given a title, *theotokos* ("Mother of God"), at the Council of Ephesus in 431. This title was preserved well within the Catholic tradition, and it seems to have enhanced the development of Mariology among the Catholic Church.[64]

Contemporary Protestant churches often resist what they view as excessive reverence for Mary stimulated partly by the title *theotokos* or by the Apostles' Creed, "born of Virgin Mary *(natus ex Maria virgine)*,"[65] which is incidentally in the Chalcedonian Definition, "born of Mary the Mother of God." Certainly, the avoidance of her reverence is in part motivated by the fear that such an attitude may cross the line between authentic faith and superstitious beliefs, which by the way is also a concern of *Lumen Gentium* (8.52-69). It may not be proper to think, however, that the motherly involvement in the divine plan of salvation expressed in the Scripture may be readily neglected in the search for "authenticity." The confession of the Marian origin of the Son of God is more than a tool to defend the christological teaching that divinity and humanity are one in the person of Jesus.[66] The motherly involvement in the history of salvation can impress the assertion of the full worth of those who have been largely underestimated in the patriarchal history of humankind.[67] Theology that embraces the fuller expression of who God is helps to enhance an authentic experience among all members of the church and to invite into that experience people of all cultures, even the one that Ferreira in *Silence* declared incapable of accepting or being accepted by "Father God."

A culture with perhaps a pathological longing for maternal dealing still presents a perspective that may be lacking in comparison to the cultures that have long oligopolized the exegesis of Scripture. The cultural reading of the text with the particular perspective may have a place in the attempt to reach toward a yet fuller experience of God.

---

63. Sasagu Arai, *Shinyaku Seisho No Josei Kan* ["New Testament perspectives on women"] (Tokyo: Iwanami, 1988), pp. 283-320. See Johnson, *She Who Is*, pp. 50-54.

64. See articles 53 and 66 of *Lumen Gentium (Dogmatic Constitution of the Church)*.

65. Jan Milič Lochman, *Das Glaubensbekenntnis, Grundriß der Dogmatik im Anschluß an das Credo*, 2nd ed. (Gütersloh: Mohn, 1982), p. 88.

66. Tyrannius Rufinus, *A Commentary on the Apostles' Creed*, trans. J. N. D. Kelly (Westminster: Newman; London: Longmans, 1955), pp. 42-47.

67. Lochman, *Das Glaubensbekenntnis*, p. 97.

When the author of *Silence* read Luke 22:61, he saw his mother's tears in Jesus' stare at Peter in his denial at the high priest's courtyard.[68] The recognizable gap between the male and the female figures could only be filled by a novelist's instinct, yet the instinct should not be disregarded as a subjective hindrance to the science of exegesis. Exegesis is after all said to be both science and art.[69] One would do well to attend to the rather quiet, if not silent, motherly whisper in the Scripture.

Reading List

Atsuhiro Asano, *Community-Identity Construction in Galatians*, JSNTSup 285 (London: T&T Clark, 2005).

Takeo Doi, *The Anatomy of Dependence*, trans. John Bester (Tokyo: Kodansha, 1973).

Suzan Eastman, *Recovering Paul's Mother Tongue: Language and Theology in Galatians* (Grand Rapids: Eerdmans, 2007).

Shusaku Endo, *Silence*, trans. William Johnston (Rutland: Tuttle, 1969).

Beverly Roberts Gaventa, *Our Mother Saint Paul* (Louisville: Westminster John Knox, 2007).

Brigitte Kahl, "No Longer Male: Masculinity Struggles behind Galatians 3:28?" *JSNT* 79 (2000): 37-49.

Sallie McFague, *Metaphorical Theology: Models of God in Religious Language* (Philadelphia: Fortress, 1982).

Phyllis Trible, *God and the Rhetoric of Sexuality*, Overtures to Biblical Theology (Philadelphia: Fortress, 1979).

68. Endo, "Gariraya No Haru" ["Spring in Galilee"], in *Haha Naru Mono* ["Motherliness"], p. 167.

69. Darrell Bock and Buist Fanning, *Interpreting the New Testament: Introduction to the Art and Science of Exegesis* (Wheaton: Crossway, 2006), p. 17.

CHAPTER 8

How to Understand a Biblical God in Chinese: Toward a Cross-Cultural Biblical Hermeneutics

ZI WANG

ABSTRACT

This paper seeks to study the challenges of translating the term and names of the biblical God in Confucianist (linguistic context) China and to answer this question: what is the relationship between Chinese culture (in particular, Confucianist culture) and the universal claims of Christianity? First, this essay will review the historical debates regarding various translations for the names of God *(Shin, Shang-ti)* used by Western missionaries (Catholic and Protestant), and subsequently the printed versions of Chinese Bibles. The sociopolitical context of the missionaries will be considered, with a focus on how the gospel was (mis)communicated to the Chinese people.

Indeed, the relationship between Christian faith and Chinese culture is the core issue in the translation of God's name(s). This essay will analyze the conflict between them, explore the process by which the translations were integrated, and propose a cross-cultural biblical hermeneutics that focuses on a "fusion of horizons" as a way to avoid miscommunication and misunderstanding. The essay will draw on a reading of Romans (esp. 1:16-17) in dialogue with a Chinese understanding of the biblical God.

How does one accurately express the understanding of the Christian/biblical God in Chinese? Do we use the term *Shang-ti* or *Shin*? Or do we use other names? The terminology question became the focus of debate as early as the time of the arrival of Christianity in China. In the subsequent few hundred years, it has been intermittently discussed, and the question is not fully resolved even today. In fact, using *Shang-ti* to refer to the biblical God has long been a popular practice. When talking about *Shang-ti,* the vast majority of Chinese people think of the highest Christian Master. However, among Chinese and Western scholars, the issue is complex because behind the term is a conflict between Christianity and Chinese cultures. Therefore it is directly related to the complex history of the spread of Christianity in China. As the representative of Chinese traditional culture, Confucianism is highly relational (family and society) and particular (heaven, humanity, earth). What is the relationship between this Confucianist culture and the universal claims of Christianity? What kind of impact will this relationship have on the further understanding of the Christian doctrine of God in the Chinese context?

This essay will first briefly survey the doctrine of the Trinity/God in Chinese church history. Second, it will examine the history of "the term question," with special attention to how the interpretation of the Bible has shaped the way people envision the relationship between Chinese traditional culture and the Christian faith. Then the essay will try to respond to the term question from the perspective of a cross-cultural interpretation of the Bible, which is based on the description of the concept of *Shang-ti*/Heaven in the cultural context of Chinese people encountering the Christian faith. It will also attempt to understand the concept of God in Rom. 1:16-17 as an example of the possibilities for dialogue and translation in moving toward a better interaction between Christian faith and Chinese culture.

I. Chinese Christian Understandings of Trinity/God

The effort to understand and proclaim the biblical God in the Chinese context, or to build up Chinese indigenous theology, has been the pursuit of several generations of Chinese scholars and Christians. Notwithstanding, it is still a work in progress, and many church leaders, theologians, and scholars in China have made their own contributions in various ways.

Some preachers from the field of Chinese pragmatic ethics are more concerned with Christians' practical lives rather than the logical analysis of doctrine. Ni Tuo-sheng (Watchman Nee, 1903-1972), for example, did not pay much attention to Christology or the Trinity in his theology, but devoted himself to the spiritual life and building up the local churches. He stressed the centrality of Christ in the doctrines of Christianity, believing that the aim of God's creation was solely to display Christ's glory, and he believed Christ to be the center of the Godhead,[1] while God revealed himself in Christ and humans become God's sons and daughters in Christ. Accordingly, what Christians should do is to live out the life of Christ.

Also, Zhao Zi-chen (1888-1979), one of the most influential theologians of the twentieth century in China, is the initiator of Chinese contextualizing theology. He devoted himself to interpreting the Christian faith in a Chinese cultural context in an effort to accommodate the tradition to believers' lives. One can hardly find a description of God as omniscient, omnipresent, or omnipotent in his writings. Zhao preferred to introduce a personal God. He thought God was the purest and most perfect standard of personality.[2]

Both Wu Yao-zong (1893-1979), the founder of the Three-Self patriotic movement of Chinese Christianity, and Ding Guang-xun (1915-2012), an outstanding leader of the church in China, are representatives of liberal Christianity (modernist). Wu Yao-zong believed in the Sermon on the Mount and claimed that he was attracted by Christian ethics. All other beliefs derived from the Bible — such as the incarnation, the resurrection, the Trinity, and the parousia — were unbelievable to him.[3] Ding Guang-xun confessed that, at first, he conceived of God as the One with great power who is self-existent and eternal, but eventually he came to argue that the essential characteristic of God is love, which is revealed in Christ.[4] However, the representative of Chinese independent churches, Wang Ming-dao (1900-1991), claimed biblical inerrancy. He insisted that only the biblical teachings could guide Christian lives and fiercely criticized the sin of this world and churches including the Three-Self Church.

As a famous scholar in contemporary China, Liu Xiao-feng (1956-) called himself a cultural Christian, and committed himself to estab-

---

1. See Ni Tuo-sheng, *The Normal Christian Faith* (Taipei: Christian Press, 2001).

2. Zhao Zi-chen, *Collection of Zhao Zi-chen* (Beijing: Commercial Press, 2004), 1:193.

3. Wu Yao-zong, *No One Has Ever Seen God* (Shanghai: Youth Association, 1947), p. 96.

4. Ding Guang-xun, "A Chinese Christian's View on God," in *The Collocation of Ding Guang-xun* (Nanjing: Yilin, 1998), pp. 107-112.

lishing a foundation of divinity in the reconstruction of Chinese culture. Introducing Karl Barth's theology, he argued on the one hand that God is an absolute "other" and is not a projection of human will and on the other hand that one's view of God must be closely related to Christology. When people talk about God, they must refer to Christ since Christ is the Word of God.

As we can see, these Chinese believers paid less attention to the teaching of the Christian God as transcendent than to God as understood through Christ and his love. In other words, what was attractive to these Chinese is how God is involved with human life and shows people a virtue-worthy and civilized way of living.

II. Background: "The Term Question"

Early in the seventeenth century, when Catholic missionaries came to China, the question of whether to use the indigenous name in Chinese culture to translate *Deus* sparked a heated debate among missionaries. Then the Jesuit missionary Matteo Ricci initiated the idea that the concept of *Shang-ti*/Heaven in Confucian classics corresponded to the concept of the Catholic God.[5] It is noteworthy that when Ricci first came to China, he claimed that it was unnecessary to quote and interpret the Bible when discussing *Deus* with the Chinese (especially the monks or literati), because the authority of the Bible was meaningless for those who had different beliefs.[6] Ricci thus introduced the concept of *Deus*, primarily based on Thomistic theology, to the Chinese, demonstrating the existence of *Deus* through the idea of cosmology and ontology, thus providing the basis for moral philosophy. He also described *Deus* as without beginning or end, invisible and silent, with great power and wisdom, the supreme good, and knowing everything. Accordingly, Ricci insisted that it is only reasonable that *Shang-ti*/Heaven in Chinese classics could correspond to the Catholic concept of *Deus*. However, his successor, Nicholas Longobardi, opposed this view. Even though Longobardi realized that the meaning of Scripture should not be adapted to cater to people with diverse opinions, he acted just as his contemporary missionaries did,

5. Matteo Ricci, S.J., *The True Meaning of the Lord of Heaven* (Taipei/Paris/Hong Kong: Ricci Institute, 1985), p. 120.
6. Ricci, *True Meaning of the Lord of Heaven*, p. 68.

namely, paying more attention to systematic theology and neglecting interpretation of the Bible. Therefore, Longobardi also viewed the concept of *Shang-ti*/Heaven and *Deus* from a scholastic perspective, arguing that the transcendence of *Deus* was different from the concept of *Shang-ti*/Heaven, because *Shang-ti*/Heaven as a naturalistic concept did not have this characteristic. Then he suggested adopting a transliterated word for *Deus*. This is part of the well-known "Rites Controversy" in Chinese missionary history. The problem of translating the title of the Supreme Ruler in Christianity was called "the term question" *(Sheng-hao-zhi-zheng)* by subsequent missionaries in China. The related debate lasted for more than three centuries.

In 1807, the British Protestant missionary Robert Morrison began to translate the first complete Chinese Bible. But this version did not employ a unified Chinese word for the holy name *(sheng-hao)*. So in 1843, fifteen British and American missionaries in China met in Hong Kong with the intention of retranslating the Chinese Bible. In the course of retranslation, these missionaries disagreed on how to translate *elohim* and *theos*. A group dominated by British missionaries insisted on the old translation of *Shang-ti*, while the American missionaries advocated for the translation of *Shin*. The two sides persisted in their views on this issue. The debate between William J. Boone of the U.S. Anglican Church and Walter H. Medhurst of the London Missionary Society was very intense. Medhurst insisted that *Shang-ti*/Heaven was the closest concept to that of the Christian God. He worked from Hebrew and Greek lexicons to research the meaning of *elohim* and *theos*. He noted that *elohim* was derived from the Arabic *Alaha*, which signified "to adore," hence the noun signified the object of adoration or *numen tremendum*. Likewise, he argued that *theos* in the New Testament meant generally (1) the Creator and Governor of all things that exist; (2) by metonymy, the religion given by God to humanity; (3) any thing that is put in the place of God, such as idols or the devil, when considered as the god of this world; and (4) metaphorically, those who act under the command or authority of God, and are God's vice-regents on earth, such as magistrates and judges. Medhurst thought that this connection was also indicated in the apostle Paul's expression "His eternal power and godhead" (Rom. 1:20).[7] Since

---

7. Walter H. Medhurst, "An Inquiry into the Proper Mode of Rendering the Word *God* in Translating the Sacred Scriptures into the Chinese Language," *Chinese Repository* 17 (March 1848): 105-7.

the meanings of *elohim* and *theos* were understood by both Hebrew and Greek writers to indicate the supreme as well as inferior deities, Medhurst proposed that the Chinese word *Shang-ti*/Heaven expressing the supreme ruler above all could be adapted to translate the name of the biblical God.[8] William Boone, however, rejected this viewpoint, thinking that "among a heathen people no word can be found which will convey, by the meaning which its previous *usus loquendi* has given it, the just ideas of the true God."[9] Therefore, he believed that in translating the Scriptures into the language of a polytheistic nation, it would be better to use a generic name, *Shin*, for God. He argued that in the Old Testament, the word *elohim* is not a proper name of the true God, but is a generic term applied to both heathen deities and to Yahweh. And the Greeks and Romans were polytheists too, so the inspired writers of the New Testament and the apostles chose *theos* rather than Zeus and *Deus* rather than Jupiter to render *elohim* into Greek and Latin. Boone quoted the First Commandment, "I am the Lord your God who brought you out of the land of Egypt, out of the house of bondage. You shall not have other gods before me" (Exod. 20:2 and Isa. 44:8; 45:5), to show that the Bible forbids humans to trust, hope in, or rely on any but God and to direct their allegiance to him as the *only* proper object of *religious worship*.[10]

Later, British missionary James Legge and American missionary Elijah Coleman Bridgman also joined the debate. Legge had his famous proclamation: "the *Ti* and *Shang-ti* of the Chinese classics is God — our God — the true God."[11] He paid less attention to quoting and interpreting the Bible from his viewpoint. For him, the meaning of the Christian God is axiomatic, that is, he is the Supreme Ruler of humanity. Legge emphasized that all the predicates of *Shang-ti* are such that we can adopt it in speaking of God "who in the beginning made the heavens and the earth, and who in the fullness of time sent forth His Son, fully to reveal Him to men, and to die, the just for the unjust."[12] Scholars questioning Legge's argument argued that *Shang-ti* is just another idol of the pagan world. These missionaries reasoned

8. Medhurst, "An Inquiry into the Proper Mode," p. 112.

9. William J. Boone, "An Essay on the Proper Rendering of the Words *Elohim* and *Theos* into the Chinese Language," *Chinese Repository* 17 (January 1848): 17-18.

10. Boone, "An Essay on the Proper Rendering," p. 20.

11. James Legge, *Confucianism in Relation to Christianity, A Paper Read Before the Missionary Conference in Shanghai, On May 11th, 1877* (Shanghai: Kelly & Walsh, 1877), p. 3.

12. Legge, *Confucianism in Relation to Christianity*, p. 3.

that, according to the Old Testament, all the gods of the nations were idols (Josh. 24:2; 1 Kings 20:23; 2 Kings 18:33, 35; Ezra 1:7; Jer. 2:11; Pss. 14:2-3; 33:12-14; 96:3-5) and that the sin the apostle Paul refers to in worshiping these gods was "idolatry" (Acts 14:16; 17:30; Rom. 1:23, 25, 28; Gal. 4:8).[13] They believed that, in order to make the Chinese turn away from polytheism and idolatry, they should not use a holy name of the Chinese traditional culture but choose a generic word such as *Shin*. They insisted that their mission was to help people know the true God and turn away from all false gods. The term *Shin* could make the Chinese aware that Yahweh was the true God who made heaven and earth and that the idols they worshiped so far were false gods.[14]

The missionaries who participated in the debate had written numerous articles or booklets published in *Chinese Repository, Chinese Recorder, China Review,* and other church publications, launching an unprecedented missionary theological debate. However, because the two sides could not reach a consensus, they eventually translated the Chinese Bible into two versions, one of which was published by the British and Foreign Bible Society and called the *Shang-ti* version, and another published by the American Bible Society and referred to as the *Shin* version. Both versions are still in use today by churches and scholars.

This debate between British and American missionaries did not come to an end with the two versions of the Chinese Bible. From 1877 to 1878, some missionaries in China and a few Chinese Christians continued to discuss which Chinese term was appropriate for the holy name by publishing a series of argumentative essays in *Church News*. However, some new arguments from the *Shang-ti*/Heaven camp merit our attention.[15] On one hand, these missionaries thought all the gods of the nations were idols; they believed that God's self-revelation was universal. They quoted Rom. 1:19-20, "what may be known about God is plain to them, because God has made it plain to them. Ever since the creation of the world God's invisible qualities — his eternal power and divine nature — have been clearly seen, being understood from what

---

13. "Is the Shang-ti of the Chinese Classics the Same Being as Jehovah of the Sacred Scriptures?" *Chinese Recorder* (Sepember-October 1877): 411-26.

14. "The Meaning of the Word 'Shin,'" *Chinese Recorder* (January-February 1877): 65-93.

15. Jonathan Lees, "On the Holy Name *(sheng-hao),*" *Church News,* April 13, 1878, in *Sheng Hao Lun Heng* (Shanghai: Shanghai Chinese Classics Publishing House, 2008), pp. 211-26.

has been made," and argued that, even though the Chinese had not seen the Bible before, they still would have partial knowledge of God. On the other hand, these missionaries tried to prove by interpreting the Bible that *Elohim* and *Theos* were not generic. They quoted Exod. 20:3, "you shall have no other gods before me," and explained that if there is another *elohim*, then God would not have said "you shall *have* no other gods," but perhaps only "you shall not *worship* other gods." Thus, they thought that what God meant here is that people should not use *elohim* to designate anyone besides him (see also Deut. 32:17, 39; 2 Sam. 22:32; 1 Kings 8:60; 18:21; Ps. 96:5).

III. The Biblical Interpretation of the Term Question

In the discussion of the term question, there were usually two factions: one advocated the use of *Shang-ti* to translate God, while the other advocated the use of *Shin*. However, the problem of translation was in fact more complicated than that because the holy names were not unified in the Bible. There were at least three Hebrew words used to refer to God in the Old Testament.[16] First, *el shaddai* appears in Gen. 17:1; 28:3; 35:11; 49:25 (see also Exod. 6:3; Ruth 1:21; Job 5:17; 6:4; 8:3; 13:3). This word was usually used in the time of Abraham to refer to his God. Second, *elohim* is a common word in the Old Testament rendering the supreme Lord, such as in Deut. 4:31 and 1 Kings 18:21. Sometimes it refers to false gods, for instance in Exod. 12:12; Deut. 29:18; 1 Sam. 5:7; and 2 Kings 1:2-3. It can also indicate an angel, as in Ps. 8:5; or it can refer to an earthly ruler, as for example in Ps. 82:1, 6. Third, *YHWH* (Yahweh) is found in Exod. 3:14 and 6:3, where God revealed his own name to Moses. This word expresses God's self-existence and appears frequently in the Pentateuch. Later, the Jewish people use the word *adonai* to replace it, as it is too sacred to be pronounced, and it has been translated as *kyrios* in Greek and "Lord" in English. In the New Testament,[17] *theos* has the same meaning as *elohim*, referring both to the true God and to idols. In other Greek literature, the word *theos* is employed for all objects of worship. And *theos* is usually translated as *Deus* in Latin and "God" in English, representing the Supreme Master. In English, the "Word of

16. Lees, "On the Holy Name *(sheng-hao),*" pp. 214-15.
17. Lees, "On the Holy Name *(sheng-hao),*" p. 216.

God" can be capitalized, or a definite article can be added to refer to the Ruler above all. It can also be used in the plural or with an adjective attached, such as "false," to qualify a generic concept. But Chinese does not have this kind of grammar which causes problems in translation. Moreover, the "Word of God" *(elohim, theos)* itself has different meanings in different biblical contexts. For example, in Isa. 42:1, "here is my servant, whom I uphold, my chosen one in whom I delight," the word "servant" implies God as the Lord. And in Hosea 2:23, "I will say to those called 'Not my people,' 'You are my people'; and they will say, 'You are my God,'" the word "people" shows God as the Ruler. Finally, in Rev. 21:7, "I will be his God, and he will be my son," the word "son" implies God is the Father. Therefore, to respond to the term question is not simply to choose a Chinese word with a fixed meaning but to answer this question: Is what we try to translate the world of the text, the world of translators, or the fusion of two cultural horizons?[18]

Looking back at the discussion of the term question, we can see that, from the perspective of traditional biblical hermeneutics, these Western missionaries did not distinguish between the text and the meaning of the text, which makes the interpretation and use of Scriptures appear arbitrary. They often singled out fragments of Scripture for their own missionary purposes, not considering either the context of the Scriptures or the context of Chinese readers.

The Western missionaries — whether the *Shang-ti* or the *Shin* camp of scholars — imposed their own understandings of God onto the Chinese, that is, they interpreted the Christian God as the supreme transcendental One. They cited the Old Testament (1 Kings 8:60; Pss. 20:5; 77:18, 19; 83:18; 135:13; Jer. 23:6), pointing out that God is characterized by his omnipotence, omnipresence, omniscience, and all-pervading rule and care for all of creation.[19] They believed that *Shang-ti* of the Chinese cultural tradition, like other nations' idols, might have certain characteristics that belong to God, such as benevolence, clemency, justice, and universal government of God, but still

---

18. Robert Carroll, "Between Lying and Blasphemy or On Translating a Four-Letter Word in Hebrew Bible: Critical Reflections on Bible Translation," in *Bible Translation on the Threshold of the Twenty-First Century: Authority, Reception, Culture and Religion*, ed. Athalya Brenner and Jan Willem van Henten (Sheffield: Sheffield Academic, 2002), pp. 53-64.

19. "The Meaning of the Word 'Shin,'" p. 85.

lack God's essential characteristics.[20] First, God is the eternally self-existent One. When Moses asked for God's name in the Exodus text, God replied: "I am who I am" (3:14). The text indicates that God is the Supreme Being in whom we live, move, and have our being (see also Pss. 90:2; 98:2; Isa. 40:28; 44:6; 57:15; 63:16; Hab. 1:12). Second, God justly and rightfully claims for himself exclusively the homage and worship of all his creatures. In the Ten Commandments, it is said: "I am the Lord your God. . . . You shall have no other gods before me. You shall not make for yourself an idol in the form of anything in heaven above or on the earth beneath or in the waters below. You shall not bow down to them or worship them; for I, the Lord your God, am a jealous God" (Exod. 20:2-5). These scholars believed that evidence of a jealous God was found extensively in the Bible, showing that any form of idolatry would incur the wrath of God and bring about punishment (Exod. 34:14; Deut. 4:23-24; 6:14-15; 7:4; Josh. 24:19-20). Finally, God is the Creator of heaven and earth: "I am the Lord, who has made all things, who alone stretched out the heavens, who spread out the earth by myself" (Isa. 44:24; see also Gen. 1:1; Exod. 20:11; Neh. 9:6; Isa. 45:12; Jer. 10:12; Rev. 4:11). God's work of creation demonstrates his excellence and supreme rulership. In their interpretation of the Bible (especially the Old Testament), these missionaries emphasized the transcendence of the biblical God. In the understanding of monotheism, God is absolutely unique to the exclusion of all other gods. In creation, God is the Creator of all things and has the highest authority over all. All in all, this is a transcendent God with great power in the view of these missionaries. This power is described in the Bible through theophanies, as a voice thundering from Sinai, as the mighty influence that fills, fires up, and strengthens the prophets and heroes of Israel for their mission.[21]

Behind the Western missionaries' descriptions of the biblical God as the Most High with great power is a deep-rooted dualism: Creator and creatures, spirit and matter, theology and ethics, and so on. The Christian God as the Creator above all creatures builds up a spiritual relationship with humans, supplying a theological foundation for ethics. The universality of the Christian God is built on his essential char-

20. "Is the *Shang-ti* of the Chinese Classics," pp. 422-25.

21. J. E. Walker, "Too Straight Is Crooked the Other Way," *Chinese Recorder* (November-December 1877): 519-24.

149

acteristic as an eternal objective entity that goes beyond the world and is separated from any concrete cultural identity. Underlying this idea are two basic attitudes toward Western Christianity and the Chinese cultural tradition: (1) either Christianity is irreconcilable with Chinese culture, and Chinese Christians have to choose between the true God and false gods; or (2) Christianity is not incompatible with Chinese culture since there are good parts of Chinese culture that can be fulfilled by the Christian faith. In fact, both of these attitudes reflect a strongly exclusive mindset in the modern missionary movement in China. Western Christianity was treated as the only true religion and absolutely true faith, while the religious beliefs of Chinese culture were either discarded as idolatry or overlooked. In this case, the universality of God became the excuse for missionaries to ignore or reject the possibility of the Christian faith being contextualized in a specific culture.

On one hand, the Christian faith as a religious system is a pursuit and a belief that meets the spiritual and truth-seeking needs of humans, and it does not exclusively belong to any specific nation or location. On the other hand, Christianity also has church communities and social participation in these local settings. That is, the Christian faith has to be related to concrete sociohistorical and cultural traditions. Therefore, Christianity as a religion must incarnate in the Chinese cultural, social, and historical contexts.

IV. A Cross-Cultural Perspective on God

To understand the biblical God in the context of the Chinese culture, one needs to (1) notice the features of the Chinese term *Shang-ti*/Heaven, which constitutes the preunderstandings of Chinese who come to know the biblical God; and (2) be aware of the context of the Bible, which will fuse with the readers' context in generating meaning. Here we will try to comprehend the biblical God in the context of the Chinese cultural tradition, primarily from Paul's hermeneutics in the book of Romans. There are rich and complex descriptions of God in the Bible. In Paul's letters alone the word "God" appears 548 times, and in Romans it appears 153 times. We will focus on Rom. 1:16-17 in order to illustrate an alternative way of understanding the Christian God in the Chinese context.

The Contexts of Romans and Shang-ti/Heaven

Romans 1:16-17 is the *propositio* of the entire epistle's rhetorical structure; that is, it represents the main points of this whole epistle in a brief statement. From a sociohistorical perspective, Paul's aim in writing this letter is to question all claims of cultural superiority and to claim the impartial righteousness of God.[22]

I agree with Robert Jewett's interpretation of verse 16 that "I am not ashamed of . . ." is a strong response to social issues based on the values of honor and shame in the ancient Mediterranean world.[23] In 1 Cor. 2:2, Paul clarifies that the gospel is "Jesus Christ and him crucified." Obviously, the gospel Paul preached was shameful in the eyes of Roman society. Paul explained this point in detail in 1 Cor. 1:20-31: "Jews demand miraculous signs and Greeks look for wisdom, but we preach Christ crucified: a stumbling block to Jews and foolishness to Gentiles." There were reasons for Roman society to see the gospel of Christ as shameful. The culture of the first-century world was built on the foundational social values of honor and shame: "Honor was a filter through which the whole world was viewed, a deep structure of the Greco-Roman mind. . . . Every thing, every person, would be valued in terms of honor."[24] Status (including social status, cultural status, or even gender status) became a very important standard by which people valued themselves and others in ancient Roman society. In the book of Romans, Paul was seeking support for a mission project in Spain. However, the majority of Spain in the first century was considered a barbaric culture in the eyes of the Romans. Therefore, Paul had to challenge the values of shame and honor and explain God's impartial righteousness. In Paul's view, the values of honor and shame bring about repression and exploitation of people by people, culture by culture, and exploitation is exactly what the gospel committed to change. Therefore, when Paul claimed that he was not ashamed of the gospel, he actually implied a social and ideological revolution inaugurated by the gospel, and suggested that this revolution was countercultural to that of honor and shame.

---

22. Robert Jewett, *Romans: A Commentary*, Hermeneia (Minneapolis: Fortress, 2007), p. 79.

23. Jewett, *Romans*, p. 137.

24. J. E. Lendon, *Empire of Honor* (New York: Oxford University Press, 2005), p. 73.

The reason we can read Rom. 1:16 from a sociohistorical perspective is that we share a similar background with Heaven/ti in the Chinese cultural tradition — a similarity that helps Chinese readers notice and understand the context of Romans.

In the Chinese cultural tradition, people worshiped Heaven/Ti. According to Shang's oracle bones, the most important deity was *Ti* or *Shang-ti* (literally, the "god above"), who is in charge of celestial phenomena, natural variations, people's luck, and other gods. In the Chou dynasty, people called this god the "God of Heaven" *(huang-tian-shang-ti)* and started to use the title of "Heaven" *(tian)* more. Duke Chou (ca. 1100 B.C.E.), King Wu's brother, used the argument "the Mandate of Heaven" to defend his new regime. In addition to having all the power of *Ti*, Heaven also has the power to establish an earthly reign in realizing the mandate of ruling.[25] Confucius further elucidated the moral principles of Heaven since he reinterpreted Heaven as creator of the moral order.

When Confucius put forward the moral principles of Heaven, he was dealing with the social background of the troubled times of hegemony. Confucius lived during the late stage of the Spring and Autumn period (770-476 B.C.E.), when the turbulent civil wars among vassal states caused the decline of the royal family. The prevailing social conditions were characterized by contention for hegemony among the lords, who were continuously fighting for more lands, treasures, and the right of dominion. Confucius described this time by saying that "rites collapsed and music disappeared," which implies moral corruption in his time. In Confucius's view, restoring the rule of virtue in the past (Western Chou dynasty) was the only way to save the immoral, violent world. Because the ruling Chou dynasty embodied the "Mandate of Heaven," Confucius praised the era of the Western Chou Dynasty as the optimal reign: "How splendidly rich it is in all the arts! I prefer the present Chou civilization."[26] Therefore, Confucius understood the Mandate of Heaven as an ethical principle. What he wanted to do was to build up the rule of virtue and moral relations among people by conforming to the Mandate of Heaven, so that the violence could be stopped.

25. K. K. Yeo, *Confucius and Paul* (in Chinese) (Shanghai: East China Normal University Press, 2010), p. 115.

26. Confucius, *The Discourses and Sayings of Confucius,* trans. Ku Hung-mi (New York: Kessinger, 2008), p. 364.

Obviously, both Paul and Confucius are trying to expound a concept of the Christian God and *Shang-ti*/Heaven, respectively, to overcome suppression and exploitation among humans. The Christian God demands that Roman chauvinism be broken down and that Christ bring salvation to all. And *Shang-ti*/Heaven in the Chinese cultural tradition as the moral principle of interpersonal communication requires the eradication of tyrants and restoration of the sage rule. At this point, it is possible to put the Chinese *Shang-ti*/Heaven and the Christian God into dialogue with each other in a way that is mutually edifying.

The Relationship between God/Shang-ti and People

For Paul, God is not only the Creator who is above all creation but also the Creator who participates in human life all along by the cross of Christ. In Rom. 1:16-17, the transcendence of God is not only a universality above creatures, like that the Western missionaries pointed to, but also contains his immanence.

In verse 16, Paul says the gospel (of Jesus Christ and him crucified) is the power of God for salvation. The cross of Christ seemed to demean God and overlook the honor and propriety of established religious traditions – whether the Jewish law or the Roman ruler cult. As the cross displayed Christians' most honorable values to the Greco-Roman world in the most shameful way, it revealed the paradox of God's saving power in a compelling way. God the Creator saves this world not as a military leader or a political ruler, but as the humblest person crucified on the cross. The cross shows that the power of God is not an absolutely executed strength "over" creatures, but a power "for" salvation of all creatures. And salvation is prepared for everyone (v. 16). The word "everyone" *(pas)* not only shows the universality of the gospel's range, but more importantly, critiques the phenomenon of different groups or communities devaluing each other. Paul further explains "everyone": first the Jews, then the Greeks (1:16). Instead of the usual antithesis between Jews and Gentiles, Paul mentions here the "Jews and Greeks *[Hellenes]*." Abandoning the discriminatory vocabulary of Gentiles, Paul shows that before the salvation of the gospel, there is no special favor or distinction between different groups of people. The Greeks deserve salvation in their own right, not as second-class persons, non-Jews. Meanwhile, Paul's gospel also is different from the salvation proclaimed by Roman imperial propaganda. The Roman ruler cult believed that emperors embodied virtue in a preeminent and salvific manner; emperors were celebrated as savior figures, for they brought the *Pax Romana* to all Romans. However, the salvation of the gospel of Christ is not only for Romans but also for non-Romans. Therefore, Paul demonstrates that God offers salvation to every group that responds in faith to the gospel of Christ crucified. The evangelical persuasion is thus the means whereby the salvation of the world is now occurring.[27]

Moreover, the gospel revealed the righteousness of God (v. 17, *dikaiosynē theou*). The righteousness of God implies that God's righteousness as the whole saving activity is a divine gift being granted to humanity by God's grace, so that people can be brought back into obedience to God's rulership. In the sense of God acting in accordance with his own nature for the sake of his name,[28] we can say that the gospel reveals what God *is*. God's essential characteristic is revealed by "Jesus Christ and him crucified" (1 Cor. 2:2), which means that humans do not need to understand God's saving invitation from a level beyond humanity, but to answer God by facing the event of the gospel. This shows God's immanence.

That Chinese readers underline God's immanence in these verses relates to the characteristics of the concept of *Shang-ti*/Heaven. In Chinese culture, on one hand, the concept of *Shang-ti*/Heaven does express a theistic belief. In *Shijing (Book of Songs)*, one of the odes reads: "Mighty is God on High *(Shang-ti)*, Ruler of His people below; Swift and terrible is God on High, His charge has many statutes. Heaven gives birth to the multitudes of the people, but its charge cannot be counted upon. To begin well is common; To end well is rare indeed."[29] *Shang-ti*/Heaven is portrayed as a dignified and powerful Ruler. It creates and dominates the people on earth. There is much evidence to suggest that *Shang-ti*/Heaven for the ancient people was a Supreme Being, the ultimate benefactor and judge. But on the other hand, *Shang-ti*/Heaven in Chinese classical texts does not have personhood. In ancient Chinese classics there is no narrative about the interaction between *Shang-ti* and

27. Jewett, *Romans*, pp. 140-41.
28. Colin G. Kruse, *Paul's Letter to the Romans*, PNTC (Grand Rapids: Eerdmans, 2012), p. 80.
29. Arthur Waley, trans., *The Book of Songs* (New York: Grove, 1996), nos. 255, 261.

human beings. This is because there is no sharp distinction between creation and creator in the Chinese cultural tradition. *Shang-ti*/Heaven is itself creator and also creation.[30] *Shang-ti* not only creates the world but also is the world itself. Such Chinese pantheistic understanding needs correction from Romans 1, where Paul critiques the collapse of the categories of creature and Creator. Yet the immanent theist understanding of Chinese culture can be a bridge for Chinese Christians to understand the biblical God.

Even though Heaven in Chinese culture does not communicate directly with humans, it conveys its will to humans through oracles and changes in weather or the natural environment. In other words, by mandate (*ming*, "command") *Shang-ti*/Heaven responds to the ruling class and instructs rulers about personal virtues. For example, in politics, the authority of rulers is justified by the Mandate of Heaven; ethically, a person lives out the Mandate of Heaven by being attentive to one's moral education. Confucius stressed the unity of people and Heaven from the aspect of moral cultivation. He advocated that the person who truly serves Heaven should pay more attention to his or her own moral cultivation: "A wise and good man is occupied in the search for truth; not in seeking for a mere living. . . . A wise man should be solicitous about truth, not anxious about poverty."[31] And he believed that humans can carry forward the realization of the principles of Heaven by promoting their own morality: "It is the man that can make his religion or the principles he professes great; and not his religion or the principles which he professes, which can make the man great"[32] As we can see, Confucius highlighted that by accepting the Mandate of Heaven and respecting *Shang-ti*/Heaven, humans are able to educate themselves to achieve a virtuous life.

In the Chinese cultural tradition, there is no direct interaction between *Shang-ti*/Heaven and humans. The only way humans can respond to the moral principle of *Shang-ti*/Heaven's self-revelation is via their own enlightenment in the process of moral cultivation. Thus the transcendence of *Shang-ti*/Heaven in Chinese culture does not lie in relationship with the Supreme One outside of the universe, but in the

---

30. Roger T. Ames and Henry Rosemont Jr., *The Analects of Confucius: A Philosophical Translation* (New York: Random House, 1998), p. 47; Yeo, *Confucius and Paul*, p. 119.

31. Confucius, *Discourses and Sayings*, p. 468.

32. Confucius, *Discourses and Sayings*, pp. 467-68.

transcendence of the moral force in peoples' minds. The preunderstanding of the unity of humans and *Shang-ti*/Heaven reminds Chinese readers to note the divine immanence of the biblical God, realizing that the gospel as an event happened in human history and became the way God provided salvation for every creature. Thus a holistic perspective on the Godhead prevents a one-sided understanding of God – such as the Western missionaries had in relation to the term question, stressing the transcendence of God, but ignoring his immanence. The Chinese Christian understanding of God hopefully does not swing the pendulum to the end of immanence, but holds to both the transcendence and immanence of God.

The Ethical Connotations in God's/Shang-ti's Self-Revelations

Finally, the biblical God and *Shang-ti*/Heaven in the Chinese cultural tradition demonstrate similar ethical connotations in their self-revelations. For the biblical God, the gospel of Christ equalizes the status of everyone, Jew or Gentile, Greek or barbarian, wise or uneducated, so that in this new interpersonal relationship people will not exploit others and instead will welcome each other. The sage rule under the Chinese *Shang-ti*/Heaven brings about people's moral enlightenment, as they value each other. In this sense, either the Christian God or Chinese *Shang-ti*/Heaven expresses a similar aspiration: to welcome others for the sake of building them up. Accordingly, the fusion of the Christian God and the Chinese *Shang-ti*/Heaven prevents any form of cultural centrism, reminding people that particularity cannot live by itself, and universality cannot turn itself into a mandatory and homogenized rule of law.

In Rom. 1:17, Paul indicates that the righteousness of God "is from faith to faith." And the phrase "from . . . to . . ." *(ek . . . eis . . .)* can be understood as from (God's) faithfulness to (humanity's) faith.[33] It not only stresses the pervasiveness of the gospel but also reminds us that God's power is not only the abstract strength as expressed in creation but also – decisively – his covenant faithfulness as expressed in the raising of Christ from the dead for the sake of salvation. Paul describes this salvation with the phrase "the righteous will live by faith" (v. 17).

33. James D. G. Dunn, *Romans 1–8*, WBC 38 (Dallas: Word, 1988), p. 44.

Faith is not a cognitive concept, but an idea about how humans are to treat each other.[34] Therefore, "from God's faithfulness to humanity's faith" shows that right relationship with God will lead us to a new type of interpersonal relationship. For the goal of divine righteousness is to establish faith communities in which righteous relationships are maintained. God becomes the theological basis of ethics; meanwhile, the salvation of God is related to communities rather than simply to individuals. Therefore, reconciliation and harmonious relations between humans is the result of faith/faithfulness — as in Gal. 5:22, "the fruit of the Spirit." God provided salvation to humanity *through* humanity — so that humanity could answer God's invitation of salvation in humanity itself by being receptive to and living out the whole event of the gospel.

In the Chinese cultural tradition, the highest Master of transcendence is not above the universe, but rather is a moral force that exists in the inner life of a person, guiding people how to live with others.[35] *Shang-ti*/Heaven as the inner moral force means that in Confucian ethics, moral behavior is offered without expecting something in return, but is an expression of ethical acts. In other words, moral behavior is to seek the good by doing good. Therefore, for Confucius, the moral person would know how to choose a lifestyle of goodness. He said: "a man without moral character cannot long put up with adversity, nor can he long enjoy prosperity. . . . It is only men of moral character who know how to love men or to hate men. If you fix your mind upon a moral life, you will be free of evil."[36] *Shang-ti*/Heaven as the basis of ethics helps humans consciously transform their own lives with others into a virtuous living.

We know now that the term question as Western missionaries proposed it ignores the uniqueness of the Chinese cultural tradition, namely: (1) they neglected the Chinese living situation as revealed by the language; and (2) they had a tendency to measure and evaluate the Chinese culture by their Western religious tradition, resulting in miscommunication and misunderstanding. To understand and respect the context of both sides is the beginning of true communication. As we can see, the context of *Shang-ti*/Heaven would help the Chinese

---

34. Yeo, *Confucius and Paul*, p. 379.
35. Yeo, *Confucius and Paul*, p. 122.
36. Confucius, *Discourses and Sayings*, p. 368.

reader to understand the context of the biblical God. And more importantly, a preunderstanding about the transcendence of *Shang-ti*/Heaven as the moral force in the human mind reminds the Chinese reader to pay more attention to the immanence of the biblical God. Eventually, similar ethical requirements become a common space for dialogue between the Christian God and the Chinese concept of *Shang-ti*/Heaven. From this communication – the fusion of two cultural horizons – the biblical texts can generate new meanings in the Chinese cultural context, thus enriching the Christian faith. Of course, Chinese culture would be enriched through the Christian faith as well, since reading the Bible needs to involve a mutual process between the text and the reader's context.

V. Epilogue: Universalism and Contextualization

Interpreting Rom. 1:16-17 through the preunderstandings of Chinese culture gives us new insight on the biblical God. The cross-cultural interpretation of the Bible further provides a way to answer questions about the relationship between the universality of Christianity and the particularity of Chinese culture: to understand the biblical God within the context of Chinese culture is not only possible but also necessary.

The universality of the biblical God is not the same as the universality of God that Western missionaries displayed in the term question. In fact, the universality claimed by Western missionaries, as well as the dualism that informed their view of universality (such as Creator/ creatures, materiality/spirituality, naturalism/religion, ethics/theology, etc.), are distinguishing features of a modern worldview. This kind of universality is built on a rule of abstract homogenization, which means that only the one who fulfills the unified regulations can be counted as belonging to the category.[37] Therefore, when the missionaries discussed how to translate the holy name, they concentrated solely on the transcendence of God's universality. They neglected the event of gospel as divine immanence, which to the Chinese is the moral essence of being human.

Through a cross-cultural biblical hermeneutics we have seen that

37. Webb Keane, *Christian Moderns: Freedom and Fetish in the Mission Encounter* (Berkeley: University of California Press, 2007), pp. 9-11.

what Paul criticized was precisely the kind of absolute universality that suppresses everything particular by its own standard. What Paul preached is not a mighty God aloof from all, but a mighty God who provides salvation for humanity through grace and whose power is for every creature. The distinction between Jews and Gentiles in Jewish law, or the discrimination against slaves, women, the uneducated, and those of low status under Roman law, cannot be used to identify Christians: "There is neither Jew nor Greek, slave nor free, male nor female, *for you all one in Christ Jesus*" (Gal. 3:28). It means that being Christian does not involve fostering an identity over others: "Glory, honor, and peace for everyone who does good: first the Jew, then for the Gentile. *For God does not show favoritism*" (Rom. 2:10-11).

The reason this kind of universalism is possible is that God as the truth is not an abstraction. He was incarnated in the event of gospel. There has been an event, and truth consists in declaring it, and then in being faithful to this declaration.[38] That means God as the truth is a universal singularity. He is not a cognitive object, but a specific event who enters into human life and asks for their responses. God is *the* truth, incarnated in a specific historical social setting. This is why in the Apostles' Creed there is a concrete description about this truth: "conceived by the Holy Spirit, given birth through Virgin Mary, suffered under Pontius Pilate, was crucified, died, and buried; he descended into the death, and the third day was raised again." These details not only show the authenticity of the gospel but also convey that God as an eventful truth bears no privileged relation to any status, community, or culture, but only calls for a response from humans in their living. Hence, the gospel needs to be contextualized. Everyone needs to respond to the Christ event from one's own living conditions.

When we read the Bible from a cross-cultural hermeneutical perspective, we will have a holistic view of the Godhead. God is not only transcendent as the Creator, but also incarnated in humanity to provide salvation. In the sense of God taking care of all humanity, the Christian faith can be contextualized in the Chinese cultural tradition. To achieve this contextualization not only does one need to understand the context of Chinese life, but also one needs to respect the specificity of each culture, in order to achieve real communication. As Paul put it,

---

38. Alain Badiou, *Saint Paul: The Foundation of Universalism* (Stanford: Stanford University Press, 2003), pp. 6-13.

"I have become all things to all people" (1 Cor. 9:22). By contextualizing in particular cultures, by encountering and communicating with these cultures, and by "becoming all things," the meaning of the Christian faith is continuously enriched and disseminated.

Further Reading

William J. Boone, "An Essay on the Proper Rendering of the Words *Elohim* and *Theos* into the Chinese Language." *Chinese Repository* 17 (January 1848): 17-53.

Robert Jewett, *Romans: A Commentary.* Hermeneia (Minneapolis: Fortress, 2007).

Sangkeun Kim, *Strange Names of God: The Missionary Translation of the Divine Name and the Chinese Responses to Matteo Ricci's Shangti in Late Ming China, 1583-1644* (New York: Peter Lang, 2004).

Walter H. Medhurst, "An Inquiry into the Proper Mode of Rendering the Word God in Translating the Sacred Scriptures into the Chinese Language." *Chinese Repository* 17 (March 1848): 105-33.

Matteo Ricci, S.J., *The True Meaning of the Lord of Heaven* (Taipei/Paris/Hong Kong: Ricci Institute, 1985).

K. K. Yeo, *Musing with Confucius and Paul: Toward a Chinese Christian Theology* (Eugene: Cascade, 2008).

Jost Oliver Zetzsche, *The Bible in China: The History of the Union Version or the Culmination of Protestant Missionary Bible Translation in China* (Sankt Augustin: Monumenta Serica Institute, 1999).

Contributors

Atsuhiro **Asano** is professor of New Testament studies at the School of Theology, Kwansei Gakuin University, in Kobe, Japan. Asano received his master of divinity at International School of Theology, his master of theology in New Testament studies at Fuller Theological Seminary, and his doctor of philosophy in New Testament studies at the University of Oxford. Books: *Community-Identity Construction in Galatians* (London: T&T Clark, 2005) and others.

Gerald **Bray** is research professor of divinity at Beeson Divinity School and distinguished professor of historical theology at Knox Theological Seminary. He is also the director of research for the Latimer Trust (London) and editor of the Anglican theological journal *Churchman*.

Antonio **González** was born in Oviedo, Spain, in 1961. He has a Ph.D. in philosophy (Madrid, 1994) and also in theology (Frankfurt am Main, 1999). For several years he lived and worked with the Catholic Church in Latin America, moving afterward to a more evangelical comprehension of the Christian faith. He has taught in Latin America, the United States, and Spain. He currently teaches at the Xavier Zubiri Foundation in Madrid, Spain.

Samuel Waje **Kunhiyop** received his Ph.D. in systematic theology at Trinity International University (1993). He served as academic dean and provost of Jos ECWA Theological Seminary (1994-2007) and later served as the first full-time postgraduate head of the South African Theological Seminary, Rivonia, South Africa (2008-2011). He is also a visitor in ethics at Bingham University, Karu, Abuja, Nigeria. He is the current general secretary of Evangelical Church Winning All (ECWA) and executive general secretary of Evangel Fellowship International. He is the author of *African Christian Ethics* (2008), *African Christian Theology* (2012), and has authored many national and international journal articles.

Natee **Tanchanpongs** is the academic dean of Bangkok Bible Seminary and a pastor at Grace City Church, Bangkok, Thailand. He received his Ph.D. in theological studies from Trinity Evangelical Divinity School in 2007, where he worked in the area of contextual hermeneutics. Thereafter he served the World Evangelical Alliance Theological Commission (WEA-TC), in which he worked in a study unit on contextualization. He is married to Bee. They have two children, Maisie and Meno.

C. Rosalee **Velloso Ewell** is a Brazilian theologian from São Paulo. She earned a Ph.D. from Duke University (USA) and currently serves as the executive director of the Theological Commission for the World Evangelical Alliance. She has written and edited various books and articles and is the New Testament editor for the forthcoming *Latin American Bible Commentary*. Rosalee is married and has three children, four rabbits, and twenty chickens.

Zi **Wang**, born in Beijing, China, graduated and received a Ph.D. from the Department of Philosophy and Religious Studies at Peking University. She is a postdoctoral researcher at the Institute of World Religions in the Chinese Academy of the Social Sciences. Her major research covers biblical studies and the sociology of religion.

Randy S. **Woodley** is Distinguished Associate Professor of Faith and Culture at George Fox Seminary in Portland, Oregon. His books include *Shalom and the Community of Creation: An Indigenous Vision*, 2012 (Eerdmans) and *Living in Color: Embracing God's Passion for Ethnic Diversity*, 2004 (IVP). He has authored numerous book chapters, contributing essays and articles in compilations such as the *Dictionary of Scripture and Ethics* (Baker Academic) and *The Global Dictionary of Theology* (IVP).

K. K. Yeo, Ph.D. (Northwestern University), is currently Harry R. Kendall Professor of New Testament at Garrett-Evangelical Theological Seminary (Evanston, Illinois) and visiting professor at Peking University, Zhejiang University (Hangzhou), and Fudan University (Shanghai, China). He has authored and edited numerous Chinese and English books on cross-cultural biblical interpretation and Christian spirituality.

Index of Names

Aldred, Ray 50n
Alvarez, C., 83n
Ames, Roger T., 155n
Angelici, Ruben, 30n
Anselm, 2
Aphrahat, 137
Arai, Sasagu, 138n
Araya, Victorio, 94
Aristotle, 8
Arius, 25
Asano, Atsuhiro, 5, 9, 128n
Athanasius, 46n
Augustine, 1n, 77

Badiou, Alain, 159n
Barnes, Michele René, 25n
Barth, Karl, 4, 7, 7n, 13n, 14-15, 46, 93, 143
Bartholomew, David J., 32n
Basil the Great, 14, 15n
Bauckham, Richard, 4, 72n, 73
Bauer, Walter, 132n
Baxter-Brown, John, 96, 96n
Beale, G. K., 2n
Belt, Thomas, 41, 42n
Bender, Margaret, 41, 42n
Bertram, Georg, 133n
Betz, Hans D., 127n

Bin, Kimura, 109
Bock, Darrell, 139n
Boff, Leonardo, 4, 10, 46, 47n, 71n, 76n, 89-91, 94-95, 97-98
Boman, Thorlief, 13n
Bonino, José Míguez, 4, 98
Boone, William J., 144-45
Bottéro, Jean, 74n
Braun, R., 28n
Bray, Gerald, 4, 7, 15, 25n
Bridgman, Elijah Coleman, 145
Brock, S. P., 137n
Brown, Francis, 134n
Brown, Harold O. J., 56
Bruce, F. F., 127n
Brueggemann, Walter, 37n, 44n
Buber, Martin, 97
Burton, Ernest De Witt, 131n, 132n, 134n

Calvin, John, 31
Carroll, Robert, 148n
Castelli, Elizabeth A., 135n
Charleston, Steve, 43n
Chrysostom, John, 136
Chung, Paul S., 14
Cicero, 77
Clements, R. E., 91n

Index of Subjects

Index of Scripture References

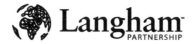

Langham Literature and its imprints are a ministry of Langham Partnership.

Langham Partnership is a global fellowship working in pursuit of the vision God entrusted to its founder John Stott –

> *to facilitate the growth of the church in maturity and Christ-likeness through raising the standards of biblical preaching and teaching.*

Our vision is to see churches in the majority world equipped for mission and growing to maturity in Christ through the ministry of pastors and leaders who believe, teach and live by the Word of God.

Our mission is to strengthen the ministry of the Word of God through:
- nurturing national movements for biblical preaching
- fostering the creation and distribution of evangelical literature
- enhancing evangelical theological education

especially in countries where churches are under-resourced.

Our ministry

Langham Preaching partners with national leaders to nurture indigenous biblical preaching movements for pastors and lay preachers all around the world. With the support of a team of trainers from many countries, a multi-level programme of seminars provides practical training, and is followed by a programme for training local facilitators. Local preachers' groups and national and regional networks ensure continuity and ongoing development, seeking to build vigorous movements committed to Bible exposition.

Langham Literature provides majority world preachers, scholars and seminary libraries with evangelical books and electronic resources through publishing and distribution, grants and discounts. The programme also fosters the creation of indigenous evangelical books in many languages, through writer's grants, strengthening local evangelical publishing houses, and investment in major regional literature projects, such as one volume Bible commentaries like *The Africa Bible Commentary* and *The South Asia Bible Commentary*.

Langham Scholars provides financial support for evangelical doctoral students from the majority world so that, when they return home, they may train pastors and other Christian leaders with sound, biblical and theological teaching. This programme equips those who equip others. Langham Scholars also works in partnership with majority world seminaries in strengthening evangelical theological education. A growing number of Langham Scholars study in high quality doctoral programmes in the majority world itself. As well as teaching the next generation of pastors, graduated Langham Scholars exercise significant influence through their writing and leadership.

To learn more about Langham Partnership and the work we do visit **langham.org**